I AM *not* A
SOCIAL ACTIVIST

I AM _not_ A
SOCIAL ACTIVIST

Making Jesus the Agenda

RONALD J. SIDER

FOREWORD BY MYRON S. AUGSBURGER

Herald Press

Scottdale, Pennsylvania
Waterloo, Ontario

Library of Congress Cataloging-in-Publication Data
Sider, Ronald J.
  I am not a social activist : making Jesus the agenda / Ronald J. Sider.
      p. cm.
  ISBN-13: 978-0-8361-9396-1 (pbk. : alk. paper)
  1. Church and social problems. 2. Evangelicalism. 3. Interpersonal
relations. 4. Christianity and politics. I. Title.
  HN31.S537 2008
  261.8—dc22
                                            2007043024

I AM NOT A SOCIAL ACTIVIST
Copyright © 2008 by Herald Press, Scottdale, Pa. 15683
  Published simultaneously in Canada by Herald Press,
  Waterloo, Ont. N2L 6H7. All rights reserved
Library of Congress Catalog Card Number: 2007043024
International Standard Book Number: 978-0-8361-9396-1
Printed in the United States of America
Book design by Joshua Byler
Cover by Greg Yoder

13 12 11 10 09 08   10 9 8 7 6 5 4 3 2 1

To order or request information please call
1-800-245-7894 or visit www.heraldpress.com.

To all those who helped make
Evangelicals for Social Action work

CONTENTS

Part 8: Thinking Politically

Foreword

Above all, Ron Sider is a disciple of Jesus Christ and a dedicated evangelical whose passion for social justice arises from a deep commitment to Christ and the kingdom. With his biblical base, believing in the meaning of the cross and the resurrection, he focuses for us what it means to live eschatologically, that is, to behave now according to what we believe about the ultimate return of our Lord.

I've known Ron as a friend and a brother since before the founding of Evangelicals for Social Action, and participating with ESA I have walked along side him in various ministries. We share many convictions, especially believing that to be truly evangelical is to be committed to justice, equity, the poor, the oppressed, to peace, and to nonviolence. As a disciple of Christ, an evangelical cannot harm or ignore one for whom Christ died. In fact, a true evangelical will look at all persons as invited into a faith relationship with our Lord. This spirit and practice is evident in Ron's ministry.

This book presents a sequence of Ron's prophetic writings over several decades. His goal has been to "faithfully beam the purifying light of Christ into every corner of church and society." He prophetically points out how, in many areas the church, that purifying light is often a reflection of the culture rather than of the rule of Christ. Readers are confronted with the convicting word of "truth as it is in Jesus."

In his ministry and writings Ron holds together evangelism and social responsibility, worship and witness, prayer and action. With the book of James he states in his own way, "Show me your faith without action, and by my actions I will show you my faith." It is this holistic faith, this pattern of behaving our beliefs, to which these chapters call us. The emphasis is on love for the whole person, a love that is thereby socially transforming. Ron is a voice, along with others, for nonviolence expressed in active love.

A relevant section of the book, one that gives Ron's writing a universal dimension, is his emphasis on family, on the richness of love and life together as families created by God. His testimony of family, marriage, and his life with his spouse, Arbutus, are remarkable expressions of love's integrity. Family is one area in which evangelicals are in agreement, even though the failures among us are very marked. Ron points to the problems of the sin and brokenness of evangelical Christians, and he calls us to humbly recognize our finitude and seek anew a life in the Spirit.

Renewal offers a corrective for all of us—for those to the left who talk of the humanity of Christ but fail to pursue his example, for those to the right whose political agenda implies a different approach to society. Our differences call us to live in the world but not be of the world, to conversations of faith that are in no way coercive, to live in the freedom of grace but in the responsibility of covenant with the Lord.

Ron recognizes that culture is ubiquitous; it tends toward idolatry and is to be challenged and enriched by the Christian presence. Any culture is the better for the presence of the church. The author of this book is calling us to be a presence for Christ, to walk with integrity in our discipleship, and to witness the risen Christ as his disciples.

I regard Ron Sider as an evangelical prophet and thank him for sharing his thoughts so clearly. It is my prayer that God may use this little volume to help us practice Christian discipleship in social responsibility. As Jesus said, "By this shall all peoples know that you are my disciples, if you have love one to another."

Myron S. Augsburger

Preface

How can I and other Christians today truly live like Jesus? How can we be more faithful disciples? That has been the passion of my life, and it is the foundational question behind all the short essays in this book.

For many years, I have written a regular column for Evangelicals for Social Action's *Prism* magazine, which I serve as publisher. Those columns cover a wide range of topics, but they all grow out of my central longing to be faithful to Jesus and the Scriptures. The columns reprinted here were published between November 1993 and February 2007.

I think that living like Jesus means loving the whole person the way Jesus did. Hence a number of essays deal with combining evangelism and social action.

I think that living like Jesus means loving one's enemies and empowering poor folk. Therefore many essays deal with peace and justice.

I think that living faithful to Jesus means strengthening marriage and family. So some essays focus there.

I think that faithfulness to Jesus requires good theology and obedient congregations. Consequently a number of essays wrestle with current theological questions and contemporary problems in the life of the church.

I think that faithfulness to Jesus means letting him be Lord of all our life, including our economics and politics. Therefore many essays struggle with the shape of faithful Christian engagement in economic and political life.

Finally, I think being a Christian means being committed to

Christ, not some agenda on justice or peace. Therefore some essays explicitly, and all essays implicitly, wrestle with what it means to make the Incarnate One the center of all we think and do.

Short essays are like good sermons: they must focus on one central point, develop the most important supportive data quickly and concisely, include a powerful illustration or two—and then stop. Short essays force the writer to get to the point fast and clearly. There is no time for making a string of careful qualifications or following interesting rabbit trails—and certainly no space for long footnotes.

Short essays also have disadvantages. They cannot deal in depth with a topic or wrestle with all the alternate viewpoints and relevant authors.

But short essays have one great advantage. They enable a writer to state and a reader to grasp the core of the writer's thinking in a quick, easy read. At their best, short essays represent a vivid snapshot of the writer's mind at a moment in time.

I hope you find these short essays to be something like a series of good sermons. I pray that they may move you to ask yourself prayerfully, How can I live more like Jesus?

Ronald J. Sider
November 2007

Part 1

JESUS, BE THE CENTER

'What Keeps You Going, Ron?'

People often ask me that question. I have a variety of answers, all of which point to parts of the truth. The most important factor, however, is simple: Easter morning.

I believe Jesus conquered death that first Easter morn. I believe the tomb was empty. I believe Satan played his best card that dark, dismal Friday two thousand years ago. By the third day, it was clear he had lost. Jesus' resurrection from the tomb is God's powerful, visible sign that Satan will finally lose everywhere. His grand design to destroy God's good creation will fail. The last word will be resurrection and new creation. Satan just pretends he is the ruler of this world. It belongs to the crucified and risen Servant, who will reign forever and ever.

Because of this, I know where history is going. The final word is not injustice, oppression, or a dead planet. The Almighty One who raised my Lord Jesus will have the last word. That is what keeps me going.

I did not always believe that. I will never forget the college years when I wondered whether an honest thinker in the modern world could still believe in historic Christianity—or even a personal God. I began to study the historical evidence for Jesus' life and resurrection and discovered that the evidence is surprisingly strong. Of course, it is not beyond dispute—by its nature, historical evidence is incomplete. But the evidence of Jesus' life and resurrection is stronger than for many events in ancient Greek and Roman history that historians accept matter-of-factly.

I will never forget a conversation with German theologian Wolfhart Pannenberg about Jesus' resurrection. Twice Pannenberg said, "The evidence for Jesus' resurrection is so strong that nobody would question it except for two things: first, it is a very unusual event; and second, if you believe it happened, you have to change the way you live."

I hope that I have, by God's grace, allowed Jesus' resurrection to shape the way I live—it certainly has shaped the way I hope. I expect to see Jesus. I believe that he will make good on his promise to complete his victory over the devastation Satan has caused in God's wonderful world.

Broken marriages, corrupted cultures, unjust systems, drug-scarred bodies, and polluted rivers are not the last word. Jesus is coming back.

When he does, Paul says even the groaning creation will be freed of its bondage and decay. Romans 8 contains a powerful personal hope. Each believer will be raised bodily to dance forever in Christ's eternal kingdom. But even the non-human creation gets to join the party: "creation itself will be set free from its bondage to decay and will obtain the freedom of the glory of the children of God" (Romans 8:21).

Revelation promises that at the Risen One's return, even the best of human civilization will be brought into the New Jerusalem: "The kings of the earth will bring their glory into it" (21:24). I do not pretend to know exactly what that means. But it at least means that our imperfect work to correct injustice, shape culture, and bring wholeness to society will find its powerful completion when the risen Savior revisits this gloriously created, tragically twisted blue planet.

That's why I keep going.

A solid confidence in the Resurrected One's ultimate victory, however, is not a cheap substitute for hard work now. Nor is it a safe bypass around pain and agony.

The Risen One calls us to labor diligently. Virtually every New Testament passage on the hope of Christ's return ends with an imperative. Paul's soaring resurrection promises in 1 Corinthians 15 end with the command to work faithfully: "Therefore, my beloved [that is, because Christ will return], be steadfast, immovable, always excelling in the work of the Lord, because you know that in the Lord your labor is not in vain" (verse 58).

The resurrection does not prevent struggle, agony, failure, even death. Good Friday comes before Easter. We work for years to build interracial bridges or construct a holistic inner-city ministry only to find our best efforts collapse in misunderstanding, mistake, and suspicion. Politicians neglect the environment, turn away from the poor, and trample on the sanctity of human life. But these are not the last words. Knowing that, disciples of the Resurrected One labor now, even in the worst of times, knowing that finally their efforts will not be in vain.

Those who understand the empty tomb can afford to lose now. They can afford to treat opponents, even nasty, powerful ones, with civility and respect. Even when they get fed to the lions—whether real ones in the Roman Coliseum or their analogues today—they keep their eye on the prize. In a day, or two, or a million, the Galilean champion of the weak and marginalized will return. In the twinkling of an eye, he will trump Satan's last card.

The kingdoms of this world will become the kingdom of our risen Lord.

I Am Not a Social Activist

I'm not a social activist. I'm a disciple of Jesus Christ, the Savior and Lord of the universe.

In the inner-city congregation where my family worshipped for more than a decade, the choir often sang a song I still love:

> Jesus, you're the center of my joy.
> All that's good and perfect comes from you.
> You're the heart of my contentment, hope for all I do.
> Jesus, you're the center of my joy.

I've been blessed in so many ways in life: wonderful Christian parents, a gifted wife of more than four decades, three wonderful children, an excellent education, and ministry opportunities that have vastly exceeded even the wildest dreams of this farm boy. At the center of all that goodness and joy stands Jesus my Lord.

When the typical problems that invade every marriage threatened to destroy what we had built for fifteen years, the commands and power of Christ kept us faithful to each other, enabling us to work through the challenges and discover a better, stronger, deeply satisfying marriage.

When new opportunities in evangelical social activism opened up, leading me to modify my earlier vocation as an apologist for historic Christianity in the secular university world, I resolved to keep the full, biblical Christ at the center of my theology and work.

21

When Jesus walked the earth, he claimed to be the Jewish Messiah, come to inaugurate the new Messianic age when all things would be made new, when everything distorted by sin would be made whole. The resurrection and Pentecost confirmed that the new Messianic age was indeed now breaking in. Of course, the early Christians knew that the old age of sin and injustice would continue, but they so strongly believed that Jesus' Messianic kingdom was upon them that they expected to live according to the radical kingdom values that Jesus had taught. They embraced kingdom ethics and kingdom expectations of holiness. They believed, as Paul wrote in 2 Corinthians 3:18, that Christians look with unveiled faces at the glory of the Lord and daily "are being transformed into the same image from one degree of glory to another."

The transformation that comes with Jesus' dawning Messianic kingdom affects every area of reality—from individual persons to social systems to the groaning creation.

At the center is personal, living faith in Jesus Christ the Lord, whose atoning death provides free, unmerited forgiveness to all who repent and whose Holy Spirit now transforms selfish, evil persons into Christ-centered, wholesome human beings. But equally important is the fact that all believers become part of Christ's new, visible body where, when that body faithfully obeys all that Jesus taught, the world can observe a new, redeemed society of transformed sinners living as they were created to live.

It is a terrible misunderstanding of what the early Christians believed to reduce Christian faith to a private personal relationship between an individual and Jesus. It certainly starts at that wonderful point, but the early Christians' belief that the Messianic kingdom was now taking shape on this earth meant the transformation went beyond individuals to society and all of broken creation. That's why they refused to worship the Roman emperor, claiming Jesus Christ as their new king. That's why Paul said the new multiethnic body of believers (where ancient ethnic hostilities between Jews and Gentiles were overcome in Christ) was part of the gospel (see Ephesians 2–3).

Every area of the created order is being affected. Forgiven individuals are now being sanctified. The church is a visible model of a redeemed social order. The power of the principalities and powers who have dominated fallen, twisted social structures is now being broken, and society is slowly being transformed. Even the groaning creation—the nonhuman world of rivers, rocks, and trees, which has been distorted by human sin—will at Christ's final return "be set free from its bondage to decay and will obtain the freedom of the glory of the children of God" (Romans 8:21).

At Christ's return too, according to Revelation 21 and 22, the glory of the nations, the best of human civilization, will be purged of its evil and taken up into the new Jerusalem, the glorious transformed earth where God will dwell with us. And the kingdoms of this earth will become the kingdom of our Christ.

Because that is the agenda of the risen Jesus—because we know history is heading in that direction—we work now to establish signs of that coming complete transformation, not just in individuals but also in the new society of the church and even in the total social order and the creation itself. As the great Dutch theologian and politician Abraham Kuyper loved to say, there is not one square inch of this whole earth that does not belong to the risen Lord.

Jesus' gospel—his death, resurrection, and agenda—must remain at the center of any faithful Christian social action. Social action without an evangelistic passion to share Jesus' gospel fails to convert the next generation of activists. Social action without Jesus' resurrection has no power. Social action without Jesus, true God and true man, at the center is not

Christian. Social action without Jesus' agenda quickly loses its way.

If Evangelicals for Social Action has accomplished anything since its founding in 1973, I hope it is that we have played our part in nurturing a biblical social action that is thoroughly grounded and centered in Jesus.

Jesus, you're the center of our joy, our vision, our ministry. We are not social activists. We are disciples of Jesus the carpenter, Creator, and risen Lord of the universe.

Visibility, Vanity, and the Media

I was angry again.

Perhaps angry is too strong a word. I was annoyed. And it's not just the level of my feeling that had changed. So had its object. I was upset with the media—and even more with myself.

One day in mid-1996, I got a call from the *Chronicle of Philanthropy* requesting an interview. "Fine," I thought, "we have a message we want to get out as widely as possible. So we take every reasonable opportunity to talk with the press."

The reporter explained that Bill Bright, founder and president of Campus Crusade for Christ, had recently been awarded the prestigious one-million-dollar Templeton Award. The *Chronicle* wanted to interview evangelicals who might have a little different perspective.

I made a split-second decision to proceed with this interview. (A mistake? I should have *known* the media wants controversy.) The reporter asked what I thought of Campus Crusade.

I started with the positive things. I am inspired by their passion for evangelism. I am grateful for the way they have led many to faith in Christ. I think their *Jesus* film, which has shared the gospel in hundreds of different languages, is a tremendous project.

Then, carefully, I proceeded with what in fact has been my long-standing critique of much of mainstream evangelical life. I am afraid there is not as much about the poor in Campus Crusade's discipling work as there is in Amos and Jesus.

"Does that mean Campus Crusade should run soup kitchens?" the reporter asked. "No," I replied. "I simply want them to emphasize God's concern for the poor as much as the Bible does when they disciple new converts." At the end of the interview, I reminded the reporter that I expected his story to reflect the positive as well as the negative things I had said. He agreed.

A few weeks later, when I opened the pages of the *Chronicle,* I was dismayed. The only quotation from me was fiercely negative. Worse, they ran a picture of me with a caption that named me a "harsh critic."

As you might suspect, I was upset. Well, no—I was mad!

I took the appropriate steps. I wrote Bill Bright, and called him too, explaining the situation and apologizing. Both over the phone and later when I saw him at the National Day of Prayer, where I again apologized personally, Bill was more than gracious. I also wrote a vigorous letter to the *Chronicle,* objecting to the distortion. (In fact, the reporter actually apologized to me for not accurately reflecting what I had said.)

So why spend a column on an incident quickly receding from the memory of a very few of you? Simply because this little anecdote suggests a temptation that I'd like to resist more successfully in the future.

I was upset at myself because I made two mistakes.

First, it was not the time and place to criticize Bill Bright. It's not that I think my original comments and critique are unfair. But there's a time and place for everything, and Bright's moment of recognition for a lifetime of dedicated service to the kingdom was not the time.

But, more importantly, I fear I succumbed to the temptation to talk to the media for the wrong reasons. I'll be honest—it's flattering to have national media call. It feels good to have one's picture in the paper. (Yes, they sent a photographer to shoot over a hundred pictures of the "harsh critic"). I'm afraid personal vanity contributed to my decision to talk to the *Chronicle.*

Powerful temptations come with public visibility. Even tiny bits of power and fame are seductive. The desire for more quickly sets in.

Obviously, I don't believe that Christians should stop working with the press. If God wants to use an organization such as Evangelicals for Social Action to help even a significant minority of Christians understand and live out holistic mission and a biblically shaped agenda for society, we will need to be far more visible in both religious and secular media than we are today.

But with that will come all kinds of temptations. To give interviews for wrong motives. To offer valid criticism at the wrong times. To distort, however slightly, someone else's view to make our position look better. To exaggerate our size or success.

Situations are usually complex. So are motives. Frequently, the need to communicate an important message widely and a personal desire for visibility for the messenger suggest the same action. One seldom fully understands all one's motives. But biblical faith calls us to seek purity of heart. God wants us to do his work for his glory, not ours.

I'd like to avoid the temptations that have come with the growth. I hope and pray that our evangelical organizations handle growing visibility with integrity. But that will only happen as a gift of grace. I hope and pray for all Christian leaders that we be kept from temptation and delivered from the evil one. I pray that integrity and purity of heart are central in all our work, especially our interaction with the media.

Reflecting the Whole Christ

Total, unconditional commitment to Christ is what I most want for myself. That uncompromising, Christ-centered passion is what I most desire for the church.

I have come to love 2 Corinthians 3:18 in a deeper way than I once did: "And we, who with unveiled faces all reflect the Lord's glory, are being transformed into his likeness with ever-increasing glory" (NIV). The veil of the temple no longer separates believers from the awesome glory of the Lord. In faith, we look directly into the face of our holy Redeemer. As we stand in his welcoming presence, looking intently into his face, he transforms us day by day, remaking us in his holy image "from one degree of glory to another." All we need to do is surrender totally, unconditionally each day, and keep our eyes fixed steadfastly on his glorious, transforming face.

Christians, who are radically transformed, actually serve as prisms: as we stay focused on Christ and allow him to overcome our brokenness, we can, like an unmarred prism, faithfully beam the purifying light of Christ into every corner of church and society. Fortunately, even imperfect prisms refract much light. And imperfect, forgiven Christians do much good. But please, Jesus, may it be more true day by day and year by year that you are the center of our joy, life, and hope.

I believe we stand at a critical moment in our society. We have been seduced by its values and norms, and we don't even realize it. I have been picketed twice in my life—both times by Christians! Once because of my stand on the poor, the other because of my insistence that the Bible condemns homosexual practice. The cultural seduction of the church has proceeded so far now that insisting on biblical principles will often be unpopular, not just in the world, but also in the church. Tragically, today many Christians mouth orthodox slogans while living sinful lives. Culture is often more decisive than Christ. The church today is forsaking biblical norms at a terrifying speed. Surrounding culture's sinful values are flooding the church. We need a new vision of Jesus for both the church and contemporary society.

To gain this we require a new commitment to the Word. It is absolutely essential that the sharp, clear standard of biblical truth be raised aloft in today's relativistic confusion and moral chaos. That means confidently proclaiming that the incarnate, crucified, and risen Lord Jesus is still the only way to salvation. That means joyfully declaring that the empty tomb is God's answer to the terror of death. That means boldly showing how the truth of historic Christian faith provides a better foundation for solving overwhelming problems like impending environmental disaster, global injustice, and the collapsing family.

Aping surrounding society rather than following biblical truth is widespread in our personal lives and our economic lives. I have tried to call attention to the way contemporary materialism and consumerism have seduced Christians to ignore or distort the powerful biblical truth that God stands with the poor, demanding justice and equity for all. Tragically, with far too few exceptions, most Christians are more concerned about living like their wealthy neighbors than feeding the starving and empowering the poor. How different would our economic lives be if we pondered every economic decision while looking deep into the eyes of Jesus?

But the church's sellout to sinful society does not end with abandoning biblical teaching about justice and peace. Christians break their marriage vows almost as frivolously, Christians engage in sexual abuse almost as often, Christian teenagers are almost as sexually promiscuous as those outside the faith. Could we behave the way we often do in our families and with our dates if we made those decisions with our eyes fixed intently on the Lord?

It is desperately urgent today that Christians rediscover a stubbornly persistent fidelity to biblical teaching. We must together resolve that we will follow biblical norms no matter what the issue, no matter what the cost, no matter how popular or unpopular the result. Being biblical means seeking to follow God's agenda rather than the current fashion. The Bible makes it pretty clear that God cares about the poor and the unborn, the environment and the family, the dignity and equality of all people, as well as the sanctity of persons, the importance of freedom and justice, peacemaking, and personal holiness. So should we.

We are human, finite, and still entangled in sin. So in spite of our single-minded passion to be biblical, we will sometimes get it wrong. When we do, we trust that other sisters and brothers will see more clearly and correct us. But our goal is crystal clear: with every fiber of our being, we seek to be Christ-centered and biblical.

We must combine—rather than divide—prayer and action, evangelism and social transformation. One of the great tragedies of the contemporary church is its one-sided Christianity, where so few congregations enthusiastically and wholeheartedly do all of these. There are some congregations focused primarily on evangelism. Others do primarily social action. Most do neither. They merely maintain the church social club.

More than once, while speaking at pastors conferences, I have asked the pastors how many congregations they know that are regularly leading scores of people to Christ and also working at social transformation. Very few know any!

What an outrageous failure to follow Jesus. Jesus' final commission was that we should go into the whole world to make disciples. But he clearly stated that making disciples includes teaching them "everything that I have commanded" (Matthew 28). That includes his hard saying that those who neglect the poor go to hell (see Matthew 25). Jesus preached and healed (see Matthew 9). He ministered to the whole person. And according to John 20:21, Jesus commissions his followers to work in the same way: "As the Father has sent me, so send I you."

. And it works!

James Dennis is one of my special friends. For several years, we served together as elders in an inner-city church. Twenty years ago, James was an angry black militant. He hated whites. A few years ago, he said that if he had met me back then, he might have killed me. Thank God, he met Jesus first!

Like so many inner-city young men with few decent job opportunities, James became an alcoholic. His marriage was in trouble, and he landed in prison for a serious crime. While there, someone shared the gospel with him, and he began to experience the transforming grace of Jesus Christ. When he left prison, our pastor walked beside him, supporting and discipling him, and James became an active member and then elder in our church.

James is a radically different person today. He is still (thank God) a proud African-American who will not tolerate even a hint of white racism. But God erased his racial hatred and restored his family. He has a good job and owns his own home. Transforming grace has invaded his life.

Anybody who thinks that the best political program on jobs, housing, and prison reform would have been enough to solve James Dennis's problems simply doesn't understand. He needed the living relationship with Jesus Christ, which has transformed the core of his being, his values, inner convictions, and family life. At the same time, anybody who thinks that being born again by itself would have been enough to solve his problems, simply does not understand. James can be as born again as you like, but if the inner-city school system offers his children a lousy education, if decent housing is unavailable, and if there are no jobs to be found, he still has big problems.

Year by year, as I struggle with the devastation of America's inner cities, my longing for more holistic churches that truly combine evangelism and social concern grows deeper and deeper. Brother James needed someone to tell him about Jesus. No social program could have restored the brokenness at the center of his being. But he and his family also need better employment and educational systems. In God's name, I cry out, "Why can't there be thousands and thousands of churches all across our world that meet the needs of the whole person in the name of the Lord we worship and follow?"

Personally, I want to do more evangelism in the next twenty years of my life (if God gives me that many years). That does not mean that I regret the fact that my particular calling has been in the area of social transformation. I thank God for that. Furthermore, from the earliest sense of my call to be active as an evangelical social activist, I resolved that I would do all in my power to make sure that a renewed evangelical social movement would not neglect evangelism or lose its grounding in orthodox theology.

But I wish I had led more people to Christ in the last twenty years. I have started to use in my own personal life, a simple strategy that I learned at the International Charismatic Consultation on World Evangelism in 1991. In a seminar, Singapore's Anglican leader Rev. James Wong shared what his congregation calls the 5-3-1 method. At the beginning of the year, each person asks God to help them identify five people who are not Christians for whom they will pray regularly. They then pray and expect that God will give them an opportunity, in the course of the year, to talk about Christ to at least three of these people. And they pray and expect that at least one will accept Jesus Christ as personal Lord and Savior.

I have used this method; I am not yet satisfied with the results. But I am trusting that I will have the incredible joy of leading a number of persons to the Lord I love and worship.

Like Jesus, however, I must care about the whole person. That means continuing with social transformation. In fact, failure to do that hinders evangelism in many ways. The poor and oppressed find it hard to hear the gospel from those who neglect their hunger and oppression. Others have left Christianity precisely because the Christianity of their childhood was so intertwined with racism and lack of concern for social justice. Recently, I talked with a neighbor who had grown up in a pious, evangelistic church in the South. Blacks were not welcome there, and social action was considered irrelevant or worse. She rejected their empty, pious religion. This neighbor was surprised to learn that there are evangelicals who battle racism and sexism and care about justice and the environment. Precisely as Christians articulate a biblically grounded approach to contemporary problems of society, they make Christian faith more attractive to many.

Evangelism and social transformation are inseparably intertwined. And they both need to be immersed in prayer and constant dependence on the Holy Spirit.

The church needs to be that central place where people who long to transcend one-sided Christianity by combining prayer, evangelism, and social transformation can come together and worship. I pray for the day when thousands and thousands of congregations around the world are so in love with Jesus Christ that every year they lead scores of non-Christians to personal faith. And I pray that because of their deep compassion they will minister to the hungry, care for the earth, and work for justice, life, peace, and freedom.

The world would welcome such a gospel, and the church owes it nothing less.

Part 2

FAMILY AND MARRIAGE

My Father's Briefcase

In the late 90s, my father gave me his briefcase. At eighty-eight years old he was longing to join my mother, who passed away three years before, and he no longer had any need for the modest leather case he'd used for books and sermon notes. And although I have my own collection of four larger and more functional briefcases, I do use Dad's on occasion, as it reminds me of all the truly important things I've learned from him over the years.

The fact that all my briefcases are more worn than Dad's single one speaks to the expanded opportunities God has placed in my path. A sick father forced Dad to forego high school to work the farm. Regretting his own lack of educational opportunity, Dad always encouraged his children to stay in school. He traveled around Ontario and Pennsylvania to preach while I have been privileged to travel the world. I have met people and read books that Dad never knew. But those differences are tiny in comparison to what I share with him—or rather seek to share, because he has lived a wonderful model that I seek to emulate, although I sometimes fall short. All the things that truly matter Dad has modeled for me.

Dad loves Jesus with all his heart, soul, and mind. Throughout his life he has sought to let Christ be the center of his life. He and Mom lived the truth of the little motto they hung in my bedroom: "Only one life 'twill soon be past; only what's done for Jesus will last."

The neighborhood threshing crew, of which Dad was a part, normally worked late every evening to harvest the wheat and oats. But on Wednesday evening they stopped early—because "Jimmy goes to prayer meeting." When Dad felt God calling him to stop shipping milk on Sunday, he stopped—even though he feared it would mean the loss of his most important income. And when God called this farmer/preacher to pastor full-time, Dad sold his beloved farm. I never had the slightest doubt about what mattered most to Dad.

I don't claim to love and follow Jesus Christ as single-mindedly as Dad, but that is my desire. If by divine grace I get even close to following in his steps, I will be forever grateful to my heavenly Father.

Dad loved Mom and lived with her for more than fifty-nine years of joyful, faithful marriage. They loved, cared for, and respected each other, and made decisions together. Their deep, mutual affection was evident to anyone who met them. While Arbutus and I talk about mutual submission in a way that Dad and Mom did not (although they practiced it in a deep, tender way), my parents modeled the kind of marriage that we seek to emulate and long to pass on to our children.

Dad knew how to be a great father. He combined love and discipline in a wonderful way. His standards were clear, and he spanked me when I disobeyed, but always with love. While some fathers insisted on sons always being in the barn, morning and evening, to help care for the animals, Dad sometimes did my chores so I could play hockey when the ice was good. He had the uncanny ability of knowing when I was ready for more responsibility, and he granted it to me accordingly. That didn't prevent me from some rebellion in my late teens, but it was a short, passing phase that gave way to a mature adult friendship. It seemed natural to consult Dad, even long after I had married and moved away from home.

I am grateful that God has allowed me to write, organize,

and travel in ways that Dad could not. My four worn briefcases are symbols of many treasured opportunities. But these
are not the things that matter most to me. I would gladly give
up any or all of them, if necessary, to be a genuine Christian,
a good husband, and a faithful father, all the things my father
has modeled for me over the years.

Dad asked me to preach his funeral sermon. When the
time comes, it will be a wonderful honor, but I don't know
how I'll manage to speak through my tears. The heart of
what I will try to say to the family and friends gathered in the
small country church where Dad preached for years is simply
this: "Please, God, if you give me the grace to come even close
to being as devout a Christian, as good a husband, and as
faithful a father as Dad has been, I will be forever grateful.
And if someday one of my sons or daughter should preach
my funeral sermon, please help me live so they can say the
same thing about me."

Living Between Christmas and Easter

One year when our August vacation time had arrived, instead of heading to our beloved spot in Maine, we drove to Ontario to spend several days with my failing, elderly father. We needed to share some of the pain and struggle that attacks us all between Christmas and Easter.

Christmas declares the worth and splendor of creation, and probably nothing affirms the sheer goodness of the created world as vividly as the incarnation, when the eternal Son became flesh. The Maine cabin along Nicatous Lake that my wife, Arbutus, and I share with two other partners is one of our favorite symbols of creation and splendor. Every visit relaxes and refreshes, and Arbutus and I always enjoy unusual delight together: blue sky with floating clouds, spectacular sunsets over the lake, soaring eagles, calling loons, dancing waves, and silent, peaceful nights. In fact, I conceived this column early on a Sunday morning as the cool lake breezes wafted through our cabin windows, and I lay with my arms wrapped closely around my sleeping sweetheart.

Arbutus and I love this special spot in Maine and treasure it as a reminder of the goodness of life, so it is not surprising that we chose to celebrate our fortieth wedding anniversary this year at the cabin. All our children came—for good food, water skiing, berry picking, fishing, and great talks. Earthly life, the incarnation tells us, is very good indeed.

More amazing, Easter promises that things get even better.

Human life does not vanish, disappearing forever after a few short decades. The risen Lord promises to return and raise us from the dead to sing and dance with him eternally. All that is good in this life will continue, however transformed. Revelation 21–22 declare that the best of human civilization—"the glory of the nations"—will be purged of evil and participate in the New Jerusalem. We delight in the glories of creation during our three-score years and ten, knowing that something even better awaits us after death.

After death. There's the rub. Good Friday comes between Christmas and Easter, and during this time agony and struggle compete with joy and delight. One of *Prism*'s former editors, Dwight Ozard, struggles hard with unexpected cancer that threatens a young marriage and the plans and contributions of a gifted young leader. When I called Elsie Kipfer to ask if we could again stay in their basement guestroom while we visited my dad, she sadly told me that her just-retired husband had advanced cancer. Just two months ago, when we had stayed there on a previous visit, they had no inkling of a secret destroyer at work in Levi's body.

Watching my dad descend into disability, weakness, and pain is a sharp reminder that agony is a part of this life. After more than eighty-five years of good health, almost sixty years of marriage, and decades of fruitful ministry, my dad is slowly dying. He struggles for breath. He walks with difficulty, back bent way forward, leaning on his cane. While I was there, he reluctantly reached the painful but necessary decision to accept the indignity of allowing the nursing staff to help him dress.

Every night brings anxiety. Mini heart attack after mini heart attack brings the panic of gasping for breath. Water pills allegedly help, but the result is frequent trips to the bathroom and an occasional embarrassment.

Even now, Dad is a wonderful model of Christian integrity. He does not complain. He treats everyone, including the constant stream of nurses, aides, and doctors, with thoughtfulness and kindness. Constantly, he prays for family and friends. Dad is teaching me so much about how to grow old as a faithful Christian.

But Dad is sad now. He misses Mom, who died three years ago. Every night brings the fear of new attacks. Every day is just a series of slow shuffles to the toilet and three wheelchair rides to the dining room for food that my weakening dad does not really want.

Of course Dad knows that Easter is coming. He longs to go home, and all his children pray that it may be soon. His faith is strong. He is eager to see Mother on the other shore, but the passage across the Jordan is difficult and frightening. Yes, the Good Shepherd is with us even in the valley of the shadow of death, but we were not created for the slow, creeping agony that my dying dad now battles.

My bent, fragile father is for me the most vivid reminder that we live between Christmas and Easter, where pain and struggle enter even the most joyful, happy, Spirit-filled lives. Christians, too, must face this reality in all its awful ugliness.

But we do not let it overshadow Christmas and Easter. Life now is full of ecstasy and beauty. Gorgeous August sunsets abound, like the one slowly sinking into quiet Nicatous Lake as I finish this article. Joy and wholeness, like that enjoyed by my dad for almost sixty years of happy marriage and seventy-five years of walking with Christ, are what the incarnation at Christmas is all about. And Easter promises that after a short moment of pain and, yes, terror, the glorious goodness continues in a new key forever.

Twice Helpless, Always Beloved

I sat down in the rocker so I could hold her with total safety. Then my son gently placed his six-week-old daughter in Grandpa's eager arms.

I held her softly, rocked her slowly, and gazed with joy and awe at the tiny, soft bundle of new life: my first grandchild. Anastasia Eloise Sider-Rose—truly flesh of my flesh and bone of my bone—at least one-quarter of her.

I held Ana many times in those next few days while Arbutus and I visited Chicago to see her for the first time. I often prayed quietly, thanking God for Ana's safe arrival to wonderful parents in a wealthy country where she can grow up enjoying an abundance of food, healthcare, education—opportunities unimaginable for half the world's babies born the same day. I prayed that she would grow up to know and love the Lord, that God would protect her from the many evils that stalk this world, and that God would lead her to a Christian husband who would love and treasure her as much as her father does her mother.

But even as I dreamed about the brilliant, godly woman this tiny child will become, what was most obvious was her total helplessness. She depends on her mother and father for everything, and when she has some undefined distress (usually a raving hunger for Mom's satisfying milk) she can only signal it by crying incoherently.

Both before and after my trip to Chicago, I traveled to

Ontario to see my ninety-year-old father. Dad has had a wonderful life as a successful farmer, a dedicated pastor, a loving and wise father and grandfather. But today he is almost as helpless as his newest great-granddaughter.

Dad spends virtually all his time in bed now, dependent on others to dress and undress him, push his wheelchair to and from the dining room for meals, and sometimes even help him go to the bathroom.

When I arrived he was eager to sit up in his wheelchair to talk. But after just fifteen minutes, he apologized that he was too tired and needed to lie back down again. He slept much of the time I was there.

In spite of his frail condition, Dad had made sure he obtained a New Testament for Ana, wanting to continue the tradition that he and Mom started years ago of giving the Good News to every great-grandchild. Dad knows the most important treasure he can pass on to his family.

Until very recently, he prayed every day by name for all his children, grandchildren, and great-grandchildren as well as his local church and scores of missionaries. But now he says:"I don't even have strength to pray much anymore."

Dad so much longs to go home to be with Jesus—and his darling wife who went to heaven five years before. He cannot understand why the Lord leaves him here in pain and helplessness rather than take him now.

Dad's trust in God is remarkable and robust, but being so frail in body is very difficult for him. In one telephone conversation he wept as he spoke of his weak body and failing memory. Please, Jesus, take him soon.

Both Dad and Ana reflect the mystery of life, which begins, and often ends, in total helplessness. At both ends of life, we are obliged to depend completely on the care of others. For Ana and Dad, that support is strong, loving, and secure. But for so many in our world, it is fragile and inadequate. For our family, friends, and neighbors at either end of life, we are summoned to incarnate our belief in the sanctity of human life, no matter how frail or untenable it might be.

When I described Dad's situation to a non-Christian friend, his response was "You can see why people demand the right to end their life before they become so helpless."

I was glad Dad does not demand that "right." He has signed all the necessary papers so that when the next heart attack or life-threatening situation occurs, doctors and nurses will refrain from taking measures to save his life or keep him alive artificially. But beyond that, he trusts that God knows better than he does when his life on earth should end.

Dad's weakness and pain moved me to tears. Ana's very presence and first smile brought me breathtaking joy. It's mystifying to be dealing with both experiences simultaneously. But Ana's name—Anastasia means "resurrection" in Greek—provides the central clue to understanding this God-ordained cycle of life. Ana, God willing, will soon grow out of her helplessness and enjoy decades of strength, mature interdependence, and faithful service in Christ's kingdom. But one day, when she is once again helpless, as Dad is today, her name will remind her that life has really only just begun. For on the other side of death's dark valley is life eternal in the presence of the Resurrected One.

The Awesome Goodness of Human Love: A Meditation at Christmas

Most summers Arbutus and I spend several wonderful weeks at our little spot along Nicatous Lake in northern Maine. This time of happiness and mutual delight in each other moves me to reflect on the awesome goodness of human love.

Arbutus and I simply love being together. That's true all—well, almost all—the time, and especially at our cabin on Nicatous Lake. I suppose it is especially easy to be romantic lovers at that gorgeous spot. There is no need for TV, restaurants, or expensive things. The simple things of life are more than enough. For several weeks, we sleep as long as we want; we make meals together; I fish every day; we read as much or as little of whatever we want; and we pick wild raspberries, blueberries, and blackberries (gallons of them some years). It's great when friends drop by for a visit, but we enjoy just being together so much that even if nobody comes, the two of us have a wonderful time together. I am simply amazed at how much joy a couple our age can experience together.

I don't mean to overstate things. Of course, we still sometimes disagree, quarrel, and hurt each other. But mostly we feel incredibly blessed with a quiet, pervasive happiness.

Our experience is just one tiny personal example of the wondrous gift of human love that flourishes all over the planet. Watching our son and daughter-in-law lovingly care for and delight in our grandchildren reminds us of the hundreds of millions of parents who sacrifice for their children and discover great joy in them. Hundreds of millions of adult children care, even at great inconvenience, for elderly parents. Millions of neighbors share generously with those in need.

Of course, there is another side. Hundreds of millions of families experience pain and anguish—from illness, famine, war, and the selfish choices of spouses, parents, neighbors.

Once, a good friend in our small group expressed her deep anger at God for allowing all the evil in the world. To her, at least at the moment, the glass is more than half empty. So much—in the world, the United States, our broken city neighborhoods, our families—is misguided, wrong, painful, and vicious. She is partly right. There is enormous evil around.

Frankly, I do not know what the balance is. More evil than good? More love than hate? I am inclined to embrace the positive conclusion.

Whatever the balance, there is a vast amount of human love in the world—hundreds of millions of parents truly delighting in their children and hundreds of millions of husbands and wives genuinely caring for each other. Even in the midst of great evil and enormous hardship, billions of people every day find delight in the goodness of human love. And, less often, but still in large numbers, there are married couples that have truly sought to live according to the Creator's commands and have discovered, as a result, deep, abiding mutual love that is truly astonishing in its beauty and goodness.

I am sure the Creator of the galaxies, who chose to become a baby at Christmas so long ago, is pleased. His birth brought great joy to his mother and her husband. He grew up surrounded by the love of caring parents, adding to their joy by his obedience. As an adult he developed deep friendships with men and women. On the cross, when evil did its worst, he lovingly asked John to take care of his mother. Nothing reveals how much God delights in the awesome goodness of human love so clearly as the incarnation. The Creator of the universe personally experienced in our very flesh and blood not only the worst of human hate but also the best of human love.

At Christmas, God willing, as Arbutus and I celebrate Christ's coming surrounded by our children and grandchildren, we will give thanks that God has given us the awesome gift of human love—for each other, our children, their children, and many dear friends. And we will pray for the grace and strength to continue working to correct injustice and restore the broken, so that many more of God's children can enjoy the goodness of human love.

Wedded Witness

Heartbreak and agony stalk America's homes. The divorce rate continues to climb, taking its toll on both adults and children.

What can be done? Public policies that penalize marriage need to be changed. And the media need to stop glorifying sexual promiscuity. But something else is even more important.

What if Christians lived joyful, fulfilling marriages right in the midst of our society's marital hell? By modeling marriages full of joy and wholeness, we could offer a hurting world a powerfully attractive alternative. Few things would have more evangelistic power.

To do this we must receive the biblical call to self-sacrifice as we reaffirm the legitimacy of personal self-fulfillment. We must transcend both conservative patriarchy and individualistic feminism.

Many contemporary voices—religious and secular—are calling for the renewal of "The Family." These advocates agree on much of the agenda as it relates to children, but both the religious and the secular groups find the nature of the wife/husband relationship a stickier, more difficult matter.

We are caught between two conflicting values—the value of lifelong marriage covenant and commitment to stable families on the one hand, and on the other the value of individual freedom that says each person, male and female, ought to be free to pursue their own dreams, gifts, career. Both American culture and the Christian church are searching for a balance between these two conflicting loyalties.

Our culture has in the last two generations sacrificed family stability on the altar of personal freedom. Some conservative Christian groups seem quite willing to sacrifice the freedom of women for the sake of stable homes.

How tragic that the church too often settles for an either/or approach. Legitimate individual fulfillment need not be sacrificed on the altar of "family values," nor does the nurture and care of children need to be sacrificed on the altar of selfish individualism.

The reality is, we will never renew family life unless we can develop joyful, faithful, and fulfilling marriage relationships. To do that, however, we must transcend both conservative patriarchy and individualistic feminism. We must recover the biblical call to self-sacrifice as we reaffirm a legitimate concern for personal fulfillment.

Individual dignity and worth, freedom and equality—for women as well as men—flow directly and consistently from biblical revelation.

Jesus emphasized the value of each individual and modeled a radically new dignity and equality for women. He swept aside old traditions that taught men not to appear in public with women and considered it better to burn a copy of the Torah than to let a woman touch it. Jesus traveled with women (see Luke 8:1-3), allowed a former prostitute to kiss his feet in public, and taught Mary theology. Women in the primitive church clearly participated in astonishing new ways in prayer, service, and ministry. St. Paul's instructions to husbands and wives begin with a revolutionary call to mutual submission: "Submit to one another out of reverence for Christ" (Ephesians 5:21 NIV). His ringing declaration in Galatians 3:28 that in Christ "there is neither Jew nor Greek, slave nor free, male nor female" (NIV) sounds like a direct response to a widespread Jewish prayer where men daily thanked God they were not a Gentile, a slave, or a woman.

But the New Testament is equally clear that the Christian life requires self-sacrifice for the sake of others: "Let the same mind be in you that was in Christ Jesus, who . . . emptied himself, taking the form of a slave . . . and became obedient to the point of death" (Philippians 2:5-8). Husbands are supposed to love their wives "just as Christ loved the church and gave himself up for her" (Ephesians 5:25).

We need Christian marriages where both partners seek to nurture the other's joy and personal fulfillment, practicing mutual submission. Patriarchy does not work. Self-centered feminism—and its counterpart self-centered male irresponsibility—does not work. Mutual submission practiced over a lifetime of joy, pain, struggle, and growth is just what our hurting homes need.

Christians must begin to live joyfully and faithfully in their marriages—right in the midst of today's marital chaos. The salt and light of thousands of loving Christian marriages would help to strengthen the institution of marriage in America. And, more than that, it would be a powerful witness to the gospel.

America hungers and thirsts for marriages that can combine quality and longevity. Our society desperately needs marriages built on a biblical foundation that combines freedom and sacrifice. If as Christian communities we can foster and support such marriages, we can indeed be a more visible sign of the kingdom of God among us. Our marriages can be living evidence of the truth of the gospel, loving testimony to the presence of Jesus in our midst.

It will involve pain and sacrifice, courage and commitment. The church will have to find new ways and resources to nurture joyful, life-long marriage—including rediscovering the role of church discipline. But over the long haul it will lead to abiding joy and deep fulfillment.

We pray for tens of millions of Christian families whose joy and wholeness stand out in stark contrast to the surrounding darkness. In those homes, husbands and wives know that the best thing they can do for their children is to love and care for each other. They take the time and invest the energy to communicate honestly, repent when they fail, forgive each other, grow together, find delight in each other and submit to each other. They keep their vows even in the tough times and demonstrate powerfully that the Creator's design for sex and marriage leads to enduring happiness and, yes, self-fulfillment.

Living models of that kind of joy and integrity would be a powerful witness in the midst of the pain and hell in families today. Neighbors would watch carefully. Slowly, after making sure the joy is genuine, they would often seek the same wholeness and gladly embrace the same Lord.

Departures

Only hours before departing for our vacation one year, Arbutus and I learned that our good friend Harvie Conn was expected to die within the next two weeks. Desiring to meet with him one final time on this side of eternity, I headed for the nursing home.

Although cancer had shrunken Harvie's strong frame to a mockery of its former self, his trademark smile, big shock of reddish-gray hair, and Santa-sized beard still reflected the joyful, exuberant man I had known for almost twenty years.

"Harvie," I said, "I just learned the doctor expects you to slip away soon. I'm leaving for vacation later tonight, and I wanted to come by to share my love and prayers, and to thank you for your wonderful contribution to the development of evangelical social concern."

His instant response was classic Harvie. With a smile that was one-quarter mischievousness and three-quarters faith, he replied, "I will have more exciting surprises in the next two weeks than you will."

While I headed to the wonderful little cabin along Nicatous Lake in Maine, where Arbutus and I always experience relaxation, healing, and God's presence, Harvie was going home to his Lord.

I tried to thank Harvie for his important contributions to the kingdom. As a missionary in South Korea, he had become famous for Spirit-filled evangelistic work among prostitutes. As a mission professor for two decades at Westminster Theological Seminary, he had helped generations of students embrace holistic mission. As a member of the evangelical team in the first major Evangelical-Catholic dialogue on mission, he had pioneered improved understanding between the two groups. His dozen-plus books on holistic mission played a major role in helping evangelicals transcend their one-sided neglect of social justice. (If you have not yet read his *Evangelism: Doing Justice and Preaching Grace*, by all means find a copy.)

I reminded him that many of the causes he had championed—greater evangelical concern for the poor, racial reconciliation, economic justice, urban ministry, holistic mission integrating evangelism and social concern—had been won. Typically, he just laughed and dismissed my thanks for his central role in those successful struggles.

Instead, as he lay dying of cancer at the age of sixty-six, his infectious laugh intact, Harvie told me how grateful to God he was for a few extra weeks of life so he could get his wife, Dottie, into a home for persons suffering from advanced Alzheimer's.

As Arbutus and I headed out of Philadelphia for the eleven-hour drive to our little Eden in northern Maine, my mind pondered the mysterious contrast between Harvie's life and my own. Glancing back over the entries in my prayer diary reminded me of the many times that I had been moved to pray for Harvie's and Dottie's numerous health problems. It began in 1982 with Harvie's dimming vision, a condition that increasingly hindered his teaching and lecturing. Cancer struck five years ago.

In stark contrast, here Arbutus and I were driving north in near-perfect health (as far as we know!) to enjoy a glorious vacation together experiencing and celebrating the goodness of created life in all its splendor. While on vacation we intended to review information I had requested on several retirement options. Tomorrow or the next day, of course, an unpleasant surprise may change all that, but today we face the real prospect of years of good health, deepening love, and much joy together.

Our thankfulness to God for our happy future seemed startlingly different from Harvie's gratitude for a few extra weeks—at death's door in a nursing home—while he and his children made arrangements so that his beloved wife can enjoy gentle care even while descending into the slowly suffocating darkness of Alzheimer's.

The contrast overwhelmed me, and tears of gratitude flowed. Absolutely nothing makes Arbutus and me more deserving than Harvie and Dottie. God, cleanse me of even the tiniest hint of thinking otherwise. I can only stand silent before the mystery of God's universe and his will, give thanks, and pray that one day, like Harvie, I can face death's inevitable call, confident of the exciting surprises that await on the other shore.

Devotional Snuggling*

Last night the temperature plummeted close to zero degrees Fahrenheit. Since we normally heat the house with our wood-stove, the bedroom was cold when we climbed into bed. Fortunately, that only made us more eager to snuggle closely together in each other's arms for our regular bedtime prayers under the covers.

For many years we have enjoyed starting and ending most days by praying together in each other's arms. We pray about the day's special worries and pressing problems and often the prayer gets interrupted while we share a joy or sorrow we had forgotten to mention over dinner or dishes. Together we lift each other's biggest burdens to the Lord. And there's always time to ask God to watch over our children.

Devotional snuggling also helps us get over angry quarrels. You cannot hold onto your resentment if you honestly start to open your heart to the heavenly Father.

Those few minutes of warmth and closeness with each other and with openness and petition to God have become regular moments of quiet joy and tenderness. And just a little more time for prayer is an unbeatable excuse to delay jumping out of bed on a sleepy morning.

We would be the first to confess that the warm feelings

*First published in Les and Leslie Parrott, *Becoming Soul Mates* (Grand Rapids, Mich.: Zondervan, 1995) p. 88. Reprinted by permission.

we experience in our devotional snuggling are not limited to the pleasure that flows from prayer. We are also certain that the God who inspired the Song of Songs does not mind at all. After all, both physical and spiritual intimacy were his idea.

—Ronald and Arbutus Sider

Part 3

THEOLOGICAL FRAGMENTS

Heaven Is Not My Home

I grew up singing the gospel song, "This world is not my home, I'm just a-passing through. My treasures are laid up, somewhere beyond the blue . . ."

Christians have been misled by Plato, the great Greek philosopher, to neglect the clear biblical teaching about the goodness of creation, the body, and the material world. Plato thought persons have a good soul trapped in an evil body. His solution? Escape from the body and the material world.

That is the way many Christians think about the future that Christ will bring. *Time* magazine once reported that two-thirds of all Americans believe they will be *without* bodies after the resurrection. Since about 86 percent of all Americans claim to be Christians, that means that most American Christians apparently suppose that at Christ's return they will be invisible, immaterial souls floating around in some kind of ethereal, spiritual "heaven."

In many ways, evangelical Christians have a profoundly unbiblical view of the future, which undercuts our faithful work for justice now. As the incredibly popular *Left Behind* series demonstrates, we are fixated on the End Times. As the saying goes, many pious Christians are so heavenly minded that they are no earthly good.

Evangelical political scientist and theologian Paul Marshall wrote a superb response that every evangelical—especially every reader of the *Left Behind* series—should read. His marvelous book has an equally excellent title, *Heaven Is Not My Home: Living in the NOW of God's Creation* (Word, 1998).

One of the most basic problems in much evangelical thought is that many believers have a dreadfully inadequate theology of creation. God made the world and declared it to be very good. Made in the divine image, human beings were given the awesome task of caring for the earth and using its stupendous complexity and beauty to create wealth, art, music—civilization.

Sin, to be sure, messed everything up, including the non-human creation. But God's plan of redemption was not to rescue trapped souls from a sinking ocean liner. The Bible clearly teaches that God intends to restore the whole of creation.

For starters, just as Jesus was raised bodily from the tomb, so believers await their bodily resurrection at Christ's return. But the restoration does not end with humans. Everything that sin messed up in the entire creation will be made whole (although that doesn't mean everyone will be saved). At our resurrection, "the creation itself will be liberated from its bondage to decay and brought into the glorious freedom of the children of God" (Romans 8:21 NIV). Even the best of human civilization will be purged of sin and brought into the New Jerusalem (see Revelation 21:22–22:2).

Nor is the New Jerusalem some ethereal "heaven"—it is this good earth purged of evil and made whole. It is true that Revelation 21:1 says that "the first earth had passed away" and that there is a "new heaven and a new earth." But that passage simply echoes Isaiah 65:17, which says God will "create new heavens and a new earth." It is perfectly clear in the Isaiah text that the author means that this earth will be purged of all sin and thus be so different that we can only speak of a "new" earth. There will be no weeping or crying, but the people in the new earth will "build houses and inhabit them; they shall plant vineyards and eat their fruit" (verse 21). According to Revelation 21, the New Jerusalem comes "*down* out of heaven from God" and "the home of God is among mortals" (vv. 2, 3, emphasis added). That is what we await—a bodily resurrected person living on a transformed earth in the presence of the resurrected Jesus who is God in the flesh.

Within this biblical framework of creation and redemption, Marshall has marvelous sketches of the goodness of work, art, politics, rest, and play. He also begins and ends each chapter with powerful personal vignettes and poetic depictions of the natural world's shimmering beauty. (Marshall also has a very helpful section on the often misunderstood text in 2 Peter 3:7-10; see pp. 326-38.)

Given the solid biblical theology of Marshall's book, it was a bit surprising at one point to see him slip back into the one-sided, individualistic definition of the gospel: "Through faith in Jesus Christ we have forgiveness of our sins and the sure hope of everlasting life with God: that is *the core* of the gospel" (emphasis added). If the gospel is just forgiveness of sins, then it is a one-way ticket to "heaven," and we can live like hell till we get there. Jesus' definition of the gospel as the good news of the kingdom fits far better with everything else Marshall says. Forgiveness of sins and everlasting life are, thank God, one central part of Jesus' gospel, but so is the fact that the Messianic community—where now in the power of the Holy Spirit Jesus' disciples can begin to live Jesus' kingdom values—has already broken into history. In the faithful body of Christ, we already get a powerful glimpse of what "heaven"—the restored earth where we will live forever with the risen Lord—will be like.

That biblical view of the future does not call Christians today to escape the world. It sends us into the world to begin to change it because we know that eventually all things will be made new. We now erect signs of that coming wholeness because we know that in God's time the kingdoms of this world will "become the kingdom of our Lord and of his Messiah, and he will reign forever and ever" (Revelation 11:15).

Naming Sin and Communicating Compassion

I once preached a sermon presenting the biblical case for, among other things, caring for the poor, personal holiness, and marriage. Gently but clearly I held up the biblical standard of a loving, lifelong marriage covenant. The host pastor later suggested to me that my remarks were inappropriate for a congregation that included many Christians who had been divorced.

I find it difficult to name sin while effectively communicating love and compassion. There are several reasons for this difficulty. For starters, relativists chafe against any standards claiming to be universal. Many people confuse tolerance with relativism. Genuine tolerance means respecting others and defending their freedom of expression even when one believes that their views are wrong. But it does not mean throwing out the standards set forth in the Bible.

The heart that can say, "Lord, I am sorry. I failed again. Please forgive me and change me so I stop doing what breaks your heart" is very different from the one that says, "There I go again upsetting the Puritans, but nobody's perfect, so I don't need to feel guilty or try to change."

The first position recognizes both biblical norms and divine mercy; the second does not.

A highly commendable desire to avoid being a "Christian Pharisee" can also lead to a one-sided emphasis. Christians struggle and fall. Proud, self-righteous, "I'm better than you are" Christians are an abomination not just to their unbelieving neighbors but also to God.

But is it not falling into the other extreme to say that "our sins are no threat to our witness," or that showing the world our worst will "do more for the gospel than showing the world our best"? Surely we can avoid Pharisaism without belittling sanctification.

So how can we name sin while communicating compassion?

First, let us remember that God has spoken, revealing right and wrong, therefore these standards exist no matter what people feel or think.

Second, throughout the Bible we see God's prophets rebuking sin; today they would no doubt earn the label of "intolerant bigot" for some of their stances. St. Paul, nonetheless, bluntly says that adulterers, greedy persons, and lots of other sinners do not have "any inheritance in the kingdom of Christ" (Ephesians 5:5). He even urges excommunication from the Christian community for those who stubbornly refuse to repent (see 1 Corinthians 5). If God's biblical spokespersons clearly rebuke sin, faithful preachers and teachers today dare do no less.

Third, the New Testament clearly shows that God expects Christians to grow in grace. Walking with Christ, Christians undergo transformation. Grace, after all, refers not only to divine forgiveness but also to divine power that progressively makes us more Christlike. Part of the Good News is that Jesus' new Messianic kingdom is becoming increasingly visible in the redeemed body of Christ.

Finally, Jesus—in his astounding tender embrace of tax collectors and prostitutes—is our perfect example. His parables demonstrate that God longs to forgive wandering prodigals. But while Jesus embraced sinners, he never overlooked sin, calling Peter Satan and denouncing the Pharisees as snakes and scorpions fit for hell (see Matthew 23:23, 33). And they didn't like it!

Never forget that no matter how gentle and loving our words, when we clearly embrace God's word about sin, those who are unwilling to repent will resent it. This is why Jesus warned his followers that the world would hate them just as it hated him (see John 7:7; 15:18-19).

Obviously, we must be very, very careful at this point. None of the above offers any excuse for spiritual pride, self-righteousness, lack of compassion, or failure to confess our ongoing struggles, mistakes—and yes, sins—as Christians.

My best advice for myself and others is to return repeatedly to Jesus' encounter with the woman caught in adultery (see John 8:3-11). This broken woman could not doubt Jesus' love, acceptance, and forgiveness. The text overflows with Jesus' tender compassion, but his final word to her is clear: please don't sin anymore. In Christ, compassion does not trump moral truth.

Embracing Finitude

No matter how much we have, some secret part of us still longs for more: more money, more beauty, more knowledge, more power, more of everything we deem good. The person with a decent job and a comfortable house wants to add on some new "conveniences" that her wealthier neighbor recently acquired. The multimillionaire, in spite of his wealth, eyes billionaires like Bill Gates with envy. Some of us want to be the best students, the best scholars. We desire to raise the most attractive, athletic, brilliant children—just a tad "better" than those of our friends and neighbors.

Is it good or bad to long for more? The answer is both. Longing is good when it prompts us to seek the right things in the right ways, but it is bad when our motives are selfish and we seek in the wrong places.

In fact, longing for more is both at the center of our sin and a pointer toward our salvation. It becomes sin when we refuse to accept our creaturely limitations (finitude) and frantically try to satisfy our longing with more and more created (finite) things. But longing can also lead us to the only true answer to our inner hunger: the infinite, Almighty God, who satisfies every human desire.

The potential problem comes from the way God created human beings. The Creator made us small, incomplete, weak—finite. Our power is insignificant, our knowledge limited, our beauty modest (and declining). We live for a few score years, then wither and die.

Yet we long for so much more. What we really seek, although so many of us are ignorant of it, is the living God. A God-shaped void exists in all our hearts that no amount of material things can satisfy. If the longing for more leads us to embrace God, it is good.

Tragically, we so often try to satisfy our longing for God in all the wrong places—through more money, bigger cars and houses, splashier vacations—always hungering for just a little more than what our neighbors and friends have. Sin is refusing to accept our finitude and trying to satisfy our longing for more with material things.

The subtlety of this root of sin is astonishing. Even the man with a gorgeous wife feels a hint of dissatisfaction when he meets a still more beautiful woman. The student who has been at the top of her class since grade school experiences resentment when a colleague in her Ivy League PhD program proves to be a bit smarter. Of course, we will always discover someone who is a little more beautiful, wealthy, powerful, or athletic than we are, regardless of how superb we might be. Trying to satisfy our longing with more of the same is a loser's game that inevitably leads only to greater emptiness.

Only one solution exists. By God's grace, we must accept our finitude and seek to satisfy our longing for more in the only place that can satisfy it, the infinite God. Resting in the embrace of the Infinite One, we can accept that everything about us is finite and limited.

Speaking for myself now, I am far less brilliant than vast numbers of others, less handsome than most, and far less wealthy than many. But all that is okay. In fact, embracing my finitude is the only way to truly enjoy the wonderful, finite world of creation that I live in.

Many years ago I was fortunate enough to marry a lovely,

petite redhead with a sharp mind and a warm heart. Over the years, of course, I have met other women who were a bit more beautiful, a bit more intelligent. If I had tried to satisfy my longing for God with more and more beautiful women, not only would I never have been satisfied, but I also would have missed the astonishing joy of learning to grow and love one specific, imperfect, but wonderful finite woman.

Embracing our finitude—truly accepting the fact that it is okay for me to be less intelligent, less powerful, less wealthy than others—is the only way to joy.

Finitude is central to being human. Even the infinite, eternal Son had to embrace finitude at the incarnation. He became flesh at a specific time and place as a specific Jewish man of limited strength, knowledge, and wealth. Fortunately, unlike all other human beings, he turned to his infinite Father to satisfy his longing for more rather than sinfully looking for more in the wrong places.

Every Christmas we celebrate Christ's birth. Let us embrace our finitude with a new sense of peace. Knowing the Infinite One who satisfies every longing for more, we can delight more deeply in less-than-perfect but still wonderful spouses, children, homes, careers, and skills.

Politics and Christmas

Christmas radically qualifies the importance of politics, especially in the United States, with November elections.

If your candidate loses, don't feel too bad, because the result is not that important. If your candidate wins, don't celebrate too much, because he or she will accomplish far less than promised.

Please don't misunderstand. I am *not* saying that politics is irrelevant. Elections *are* important. Their outcomes shape decisions that help or harm millions of people.

But God was aware of that when he chose to send the Savior of the world to a lowly carpenter's home in an unimportant colony rather than to the emperor's family at the center of global power. Furious debates about momentous political decisions were taking place in Rome when the eternal Word became a baby in Bethlehem in 4 BC. Those political debates mattered. If faithful followers of Yahweh could have bent them toward greater peace and justice, they should have. But something vastly more important was happening in Bethlehem.

For centuries a tiny people group called Jews was scattered across the successive Babylonian, Persian, then Greco-Roman empires that dominated a huge part of the world. This minority believed that their god was the only God, the Creator, and the ruler of heaven and earth. They believed that someday God's Messiah would appear—to overcome evil and injustice, bring peace and goodness for all, forgive sins, transform sinners, and usher in a new time of Messianic shalom when all nations would worship the one God and enjoy his wholeness. That's also what Jesus believed as he started his public ministry.

With this difference: Jesus believed he was God's Messiah sent to begin this marvelous new day. And he rejected violence as the way to inaugurate God's new kingdom. Instead, he said the wonderful, long-expected kingdom of goodness and peace would grow slowly, like a mustard seed, as more and more people believed in him, decided to follow him, and began to live what he taught.

Was Jesus' message political? No—and yes. Jesus was not arguing about the current policy questions being debated in Rome. He rejected the notion that military force could bring in the new age of shalom. He did not try to become the next Caesar.

But Jesus' message and claims were deeply political. At the very center of the Jewish hope that Jesus embraced was the expectation that the Messiah would come to conquer evil and bring peace and justice, not just for the tiny Jewish community but for the whole world. That's who Jesus said he was. And he said his death and resurrection would be central to the arrival of this new period of history.

As the early Christians reflected back on the astounding events of Jesus' three short years of public ministry, they confessed that Jesus had been right. The new time of peace and justice had begun. Jesus was—at that moment—King of kings and Lord of lords. All authority in heaven and on earth had already been delivered to him.

The big difference from earlier Jewish expectation, of course, was that the old age with its injustice still remained alive and powerful, even as the new kingdom was arriving slowly while more and more people embraced Jesus' vision and way.

And this way was political, but not in the way Rome was political. Even though Caesar claimed to be "Lord" and "Son of God," it was really Jesus to whom those titles belonged. Whenever Caesar demanded things that contradicted Jesus' way, the early Christians followed Jesus, not Caesar. They believed that Jesus' new kingdom, not Caesar's policy decisions, would be the most important fact in transforming the world into what the Creator intended.

Does that make Caesar's—or the prime minister's or the president's—policy decisions irrelevant? Not at all. These decisions greatly affect people's lives, so whenever we can nudge them toward greater wholeness, we should. Although, according to Colossians 2:15, Jesus Christ in some important sense actually broke the power of the evil political powers at the cross and took them captive to himself, we need only take a quick look around us to see that this process is still very incomplete. Only at Christ's return will all evil disappear.

Until then you and I must live out the Christian confession that Jesus alone is Lord. That means he is not just Lord of our personal political decisions but in some basic sense he is already Lord of presidents and prime ministers, parliaments and congresses. He has chosen the church as the place where his reign is to become most visible and powerful. And that means that no matter who wins elections or what politicians do, God's reign continues to take shape on this earth. When politicians are at their worst, defying Christ and seeking to destroy his church, Christ's kingdom still advances. And when politicians are most sympathetic to gospel values, they are still a mixed bag of good and evil, and everything they do is less important than proclaiming the gospel and living as Jesus' new redeemed body of believers.

I will keep urging Christians to push for wise political decisions. But never forget that politics is not nearly as important as living as Jesus' new community and inviting others to embrace his wonderful gospel. Bethlehem, not Rome (or Washington), is the center of the universe.

Naturalism Versus Theism:
An Honest Search for Truth

I frequently ponder the stunning complexity of the world through two totally different lenses.

Sometimes I view the world through the naturalistic eyes of a good friend and brilliant philosopher who sincerely believes science urges us to conclude that nothing exists except a blind, materialistic, evolutionary process "governed" by random mutations. Sometimes, far more often, I view the world through my theistic eyes, which discern a gloriously intricate, purposely designed world created by a loving God. Those two fundamentally contradictory views stand side by side in today's world. The first dominates our great universities, although substantial minorities of today's best philosophers, physicists, and other scholars embrace the second. The second has been the view of both Christian laity and generations of brilliant Christian scholars for two millennia.

It is widely recognized that these two contradictory visions lead to momentous, contradictory views about persons and society. Christian theists claim that persons are made in the image of a loving, personal God who created them with genuine freedom to embrace or reject the universal moral order embedded in the universe, indeed even the freedom to say yes or no to the Creator's invitation to life eternal in the presence of the living God.

If the naturalistic philosophy is right, persons are just complex machines that accidentally evolved. Many naturalists still somehow think persons have a special dignity and worth (we certainly are a lot more complex and intelligent) and argue for human freedom. But I do not think that persons, if made by a blind, materialistic process, possess the same worth and dignity they do if they are created in the very image of God. I also find it hard to see how human beings have any freedom in a world whose every part is determined by prior, exclusively materialistic causes and random mutation. At death, as Bertrand Russell dared to say bluntly, we die, rot, and disappear forever. Whatever worth persons may have, it lasts only for a fleeting moment and then is gone.

How is it that honest, intelligent people today genuinely searching for truth come to such radically different conclusions?

Christians should not quickly dismiss the secular view. We need to face the considerable evidence that people like Carl Sagan marshal (see his *Demon-Haunted World: Science as a Candle in the Dark* [Ballantine, 1997]).

Careful (usually devoutly Christian) scientists set to work looking for natural material causes. They discovered that the earth was a tiny speck revolving around a small sun in a small galaxy in a universe with billions of stars in every one of more than a hundred billion galaxies. Scientists discovered natural, nonmiraculous explanations for comets, plagues, and all kinds of other things formerly explained by miracle. Then Darwin caught a glimpse of how species evolved through chance mutation and survival of the fittest. An ever-growing body of fossil finds, DNA evidence, and scientific data about our ten-plus-billion-year-old universe confirm Darwin's basic thesis.

Of course, there are still substantial gaps, lots of things that contemporary scientists cannot yet explain, but is not the only "responsible," "rational," "scientific" conclusion that the scientific method will be able to explain everything and that nothing exists except this evolving materialistic world? Such a conclusion may—indeed does—force on us a painful, radical rejection of the traditional view of persons made in the divine image and called to life eternal in the presence of the loving Creator of the universe. The truth may be tough, but honest people will embrace it, no matter how wrenching its implications.

But difficult questions press in.

First of all, is there not a huge philosophical (ultimately religious) leap in the so-called "scientific" case for naturalism? All science does is show us with ever greater (breathtaking) precision how the natural, material world regularly works. No amount of scientific data could ever in principle tell us whether there is something more than the material world. More and more knowledge about how the material world regularly works tells us absolutely nothing about whether God exists. If God exists outside the material world as its Creator, God can perform miracles any time he chooses. An intelligent Mind could have chosen to use the long evolutionary process to which Darwin pointed to bring the detailed world we know into existence. It requires a leap of faith to bridge the gap between the scientific fact that a vast amount of what we regularly experience in the material world has natural, material causes and the atheist's claim that only the natural world exists. The latter statement flows not from science but from atheistic religious belief.

Atheists disagree on how compelling the connection is between the vast amount of scientific data on natural, materialistic causes and the conclusion that God does not exist. Some think that continuing to believe in God is extremely irrational; others consider the question of God's existence much more open. It would certainly be bad philosophy to argue that contemporary science demands a naturalistic worldview.

Second, and quite apart from any discussion of "intelligent design," many of our best minds have thought the amazing complexity and order of the world around us points to some intelligent cause. Even the great skeptic David Hume wrote that "a purpose, an intention, or design strikes everywhere the most careless, the most stupid thinker; and no man can be so hardened in absurd systems, as at all times to reject it" (quoted in C. Stephen Evans, *Why Believe?: Reason and Mystery as Pointers to God* [Eerdmans, 1996], p. 35).

Third, in a random, materialistic world, it is hard to understand ethics as anything more than arbitrary and subjective. As the atheist Jean-Paul Sartre said, "Everything is permissible if God does not exist." So why not rape, rob, or kill your neighbors if you are stronger and can get away with it? As Russell said, those who have the best poison gas will determine the "ethics" of the future.

In practice, to be sure, many naturalistic ethicists do develop ethical systems and argue that right and wrong are more than subjective feelings. But it is hard to see how a solid foundation for a universal ethic can be derived from a blind materialistic process. On the other hand, it is easy to see how a loving personal Creator could make a world with universal moral norms and create human beings with some innate sense of that moral order.

Fourth, there is the problem of freedom. If everything is determined by prior materialistic causes, how do we explain the inner freedom that we all experience? Surely, materialistic determinists have to conclude that freedom is just an illusion, because it would seem impossible for genuine freedom to evolve from a materialistic process. And yet the materialists often acknowledge that moral responsibility makes no sense at all without freedom.

Finally, there is the historical evidence. Virtually all serious historians today agree that Jesus was a historical person who was kind and loving but also made some pretty outrageous claims. There is even pretty strong historical evidence that the crucified Jesus was alive again the third day.

How clear is that evidence? The person willing to look honestly at the historical evidence with an open mind finds it surprisingly strong. But it is not a mathematical proof. The preponderance of data points toward a real historical resurrection, but the evidence is not so strong that it totally overwhelms the rational mind.

There is a certain parallel to the other things we have noted. Design in nature, the sense of right and wrong, human freedom, all seem to find a better foundation in a theistic rather than a naturalistic view of the world. But none of the arguments—one by one or together—represent a totally airtight case. They leave room for human choice.

Why? Biblical revelation says the Creator shaped persons as free beings because he wanted us to love and obey him in freedom, not compulsion. If God had made the evidence for his existence so total, so clear, so omnipresent that every rational mind felt compelled to accept it in the same way we feel compelled to accept a mathematical formula, we would not be free in our relationship to God.

It looks as if the Creator left pretty clear calling cards scattered in nature, persons, and human history. But God chose not to make their message so abundantly clear that they would wipe out human freedom.

We are left with two radically contradictory views of the world. The theistic view, I think, makes better sense of all we know than the naturalistic view. But, finite beings that we are, we must all, on both sides of this divide, keep looking honestly at all the solid data that human experience (science, history, self-reflection) provide. Unless we do that, we fall into dogmatism, rather than continue an honest search for truth.

Part 4

COMBINING
EVANGELISM AND
SOCIAL ACTION

A Tale of Two Churches

In the 1960s and '70s, I organized a number of seminars in the inner city for white leaders from suburban, rural, and small-town churches. Among the regular speakers at these seminars were Father Paul Washington and Reverend Willie Richardson.

Washington was famous in Philadelphia and beyond for his daring and vigorous social engagement. A prominent civil-rights leader and chair of the mayor's Commission on Human Relations, he led his Episcopalian Church of the Advocate into a vast variety of social ministries and justice work, including the development of over three hundred low-income housing units and the hosting of the first Episcopal ordination of women priests. Although the cathedral-like stone structure can easily seat a thousand people, today only about sixty come to Sunday services. Evangelism was not a significant concern for Washington or his church, and slowly the congregation withered away.

Richardson's Christian Stronghold Baptist Church was meeting in one room of a row house when I first visited it in 1969, and he was a full-time engineer pastoring his little flock of fifty in his spare time. Passionate about evangelism and discipleship, Richardson taught his members how to share their faith with others. Christian Stronghold is now a congregation of more than four thousand members, half of whom had never belonged to a church before. An extensive training program for new members nurtures a passion for evangelism in everyone.

91

"Everything we do is an evangelistic outreach," Richardson says. Today that includes a GED program, hundreds of renovated low-income houses, home-ownership seminars, health fairs, a youth self-esteem program for troubled students at a nearby elementary school, tutoring, and a Community Action Council working on political issues.

To a significant degree, the tale of these two churches runs parallel to the story of the American church in the twentieth century. In 1917 Walter Rauschenbusch's lectures at Yale became the manifesto of the Social Gospel movement, which for decades battled economic injustice, strengthened unions, and eventually opposed racism. Although Rauschenbusch rightly claimed that traditional churches too often understood both sin and salvation in one-sided individualistic ways, neglected structural injustice, and ignored Jesus' ethical teaching, it is obvious why those standing in the mainstream of historic Christian orthodoxy were uneasy. He belittled "trust in the vicarious atonement of Christ," insisted that the Social Gospel had little interest in metaphysical questions about the Trinity or the deity of Christ, and gladly predicted that "the more the Social Gospel engages and inspires theological thought, the more religion will be concentrated on ethical righteousness."

Which is, of course, exactly what happened. Many mainstream Protestant denominations focused increasingly on important issues of social justice but neglected evangelism and church-planting. In response, those who called themselves fundamentalists (and later, evangelicals) focused one-sidedly on evangelism and orthodox theology, largely neglecting what the Bible says about justice for the poor and marginalized. For decades this tragic division weakened American church life.

The tale of the two churches has taken an interesting twist, however, since the 1970s. Thanks in part to the civil-rights movement, the anti-Vietnam War campaign, and liberation theologies, younger evangelicals have developed a passion for social justice, rediscovered the massive biblical teaching about God's special concern for the poor. They've begun to define the gospel not merely as the forgiveness of sins but also as the good news of the kingdom. While maintaining a passion for evangelism and a commitment to Christian orthodoxy, scores of established congregations with long histories of evangelistic engagement have slowly developed extensive social-action programs, and hundreds of new evangelical congregations and ministries have emerged with successful holistic ministries.

In 1998, the University of Chicago published sociologist Chris Smith's *American Evangelicalism: Embattled and Thriving*. His polling data showed that evangelicals are just as likely as mainline Protestants to vote in elections, more likely to consider working for political reform, slightly more likely to consider volunteering for local community organizations, and more likely to have given a significant amount of money to help the poor. Smith concluded that today "evangelicals may be the most committed carriers of a new Social Gospel."

The story of the American church since the 1970s seems to be the story of Washington's and Richardson's churches writ large. While mainline Protestant denominations have been losing millions of members, evangelical congregations and denominations have been growing rapidly, not just numerically but in their social engagement as well.

A development at Washington's Church of the Advocate offers another reason for optimism. Realizing that preserving their legacy of social action depends in part on sharing the gospel with others who will join the church and carry on the work, they have recently begun to explore ways of evangelizing their community.

Is it too much to hope that just as evangelical churches in large numbers are recovering a social concern, mainline churches will rediscover evangelism?

Holistic Ministries Start Small

Okay, I've heard stories about these wonderful holistic ministry programs at churches like Lawndale and Rock-Circle. But how could my congregation ever start that kind of big, exciting, comprehensive ministry? The little circle of committed people in my church could never start that kind of program. It all seems too big and complex and expensive.

Do you feel like this? I know many people do, but there's a simple solution. You don't have to start big. In fact, starting small is the way to go.

Let me tell you about Jesus Action, which Ichthus Fellowship in London started about twenty years ago. Jesus Action is not complex or political. Ichthus simply posts signs around the neighborhood, inviting people to call the Jesus Action phone number if they need help. Ichthus volunteers then respond to the various requests. They help with gardening, shopping, babysitting, or just visiting. People without transportation can get a free ride to the hospital. It doesn't take much training, and almost anyone can do it.

They never force Jesus on those they serve. Faith Forster, a leader in the Ichthus Fellowship, says, "We don't go in and start pushing them to become Christians." But eventually, people ask questions and many have come to faith in Christ.

One day a woman who had just left a hospital called Jesus Action. A single parent, she needed to shop for food and wash her clothes, and she didn't know how to get her six-year-old into school. Somewhere she had seen the Jesus Action number that Ichthus posts everywhere.

"Is this Jesus Action?" she asked Faith over the telephone.

"Yes," Faith responded.

"Well," the woman went on, "I want the action but I don't want the Jesus. I don't want anyone ramming religion down my throat."

Faith assured her that would not happen. After Faith helped her with the washing and shopping, the woman invited her to sit down for a cup of tea. Ten minutes later, the woman blurted out, "Okay, what's all this about Jesus?"

Teasingly, Faith reminded her, "We had an arrangement not to shove religion down your throat." The woman insisted, and Faith shared the gospel and prayed with her.

Evangelistic opportunities often result from simply caring for people's needs. Every three months, Ichthus has a supper for those who have been helped by Jesus Action. Afterward they share the gospel. Some begin to come to the church as a result.

Today Ichthus Fellowship has a large program with a variety of evangelistic and social ministries. But they didn't start big. The same is true for virtually all the large, comprehensive, holistic ministries that rightly inspire us today.

June Kelsall operates several residential homes for abused women in Auckland, New Zealand. It started in a small, interdenominational women's praise group. June and the others began to sense a call to go into "the highways and byways." For six months they prayed for direction. They felt led to organize a drop-in center where people could drink tea and chat.

"We all felt we were capable of making tea and smiling Jesus smiles and caring for people." June is grateful they did not have to start big: "If the Lord had given us great big instructions, we probably would have run the other way."

One day a lonely man dropped in at their "Care and Conversation" center. After a dramatic conversion, he began bringing in dozens and dozens of others who needed love. From that small beginning, Dayspring has developed into a program that includes three residential homes for poor women—often the victims of abuse—and their children. Most of the hundreds of thousands of dollars in annual funding comes from secular sources, including governmental agencies. But all the staff and board members are Christians from area churches.

"The sort of care we give," June says, "is love with no strings attached. They don't have to come to the Lord, but they do!"

It's not hard to start a simple Jesus Action program in your church. All you need is a phone number where messages can be left and half a dozen ordinary folks who love Jesus and want to share his love with real people in need. Let each person agree to volunteer at least two hours per week in responding to calls for help. Pray together, and have one person praying at the time each person responds to a call.

Post signs in your neighborhood (or some nearby area where there are needy people): "NEED HELP? Call Jesus Action," and give the phone number. Don't pretend to be able to handle every problem. Refer difficult ones to social service agencies or professional caregivers, and go along the first time to be sure they get help. You don't need to do an elaborate evangelism training program to get started. After you have helped a person, ask, "Is there any special way you would like me to pray for you?" People are often delighted to have someone pray for them.

Almost any church could start that kind of simple Jesus Action program in the next three months. Usually, one thing will lead to another, and your church may develop one or more larger programs to get at frequently recurring, underlying problems you will discover as you do the Jesus Action ministry. As you develop ongoing, personal friendships with the people served, people will come to Christ. Your church will probably grow.

But you don't need to worry now about what might happen in coming years. That will take care of itself. All God is asking today is for you to decide with a few friends that you really could offer "Jesus smiles" and helping hands to a neighbor in need. Photocopy a few dozen simple notices, post them, and you are off and running.

Imagine what might happen if this year, in a dozen local churches, small teams started this kind of ministry. What if it happened in a hundred churches? Or a thousand?

Eight Keys to Holistic Ministry

My 1994 book *Cup of Water, Bread of Life* tells the stories of ten of the most exciting, successful, holistic ministries I have ever seen. These stories provide evidence that churches can grow by remaining faithful to the whole gospel—both regularly leading people to Christ *and* engaging in social action. And these stories are not unique. There are many more thriving holistic ministries throughout the world, and their numbers are growing.

The ministries profiled in my book come from different continents, denominations, and ethnic communities. I was struck, however, that they share many of the same crucial, indispensable characteristics. Let me share eight of these.

1. Unconditional commitment to Christ. This is the indispensable starting point. The leaders of successful holistic ministries want to serve Jesus Christ above everything else in the world. They are ready to pay any price and bear any cost that obedient discipleship demands. This kind of commitment sounds hard—almost impossible—but when you surrender to God, you discover it is a wonderful way to live. We were made to live as obedient servants of the Almighty Creator. When we do, we experience both fantastic joy and concrete success.

2. A passion for evangelism. Thousands of Christian churches and ministries are engaged in meeting people's material needs. Unfortunately, most seldom get around to explicitly inviting people to Christ. People do not come to Christ automatically. They come to Christ when those who serve them also long to share their dearest treasure, Jesus Christ the Savior, and therefore regularly pray for and watch for opportunities to encourage people to believe and obey him.

This does not mean insensitive, pushy evangelism—ramming tracts and sermons down people's throats. It means friendship evangelism expressed in a genuine concern for the whole person. But it *must* be intentional, and it must be a *passion* for people in the ministry. It is abominably easy to weaken and lose explicit, regular evangelism. It will not happen unless the leaders all have an evangelistic heart and regularly train and encourage their people to tell others about God's salvation.

3. A passion to empower the poor. All of the ministries I explored have a special concern for the needy and oppressed. This was at the heart of Jesus' announcement of the good news of the kingdom (see Luke 4:16-21). We do not truly know God unless we share God's passion for justice for the poor (see Jeremiah 22:16). Faithful, holistic ministries recognize this biblical truth and demonstrate it in their preaching and practice. Whether located in the suburbs or inner city, all the models I describe devote a central part of their ministry to the weak and marginalized.

4. A concern for the whole person in community. No effective holistic ministry supposes that they dare care about a person's soul and neglect her body, or vice versa. None imagines that the gospel is merely the forgiveness of sins, which one could accept and then go on living the same racist, promiscuous, sinful lifestyle as before. Jesus' gospel is the good news of the kingdom, which transforms believers' relationships with God, neighbor, self, and the earth. People are not isolated hermits, but spiritual/physical beings who live in community. Therefore, in obedience to Christ's example and command (see John 20:21), holistic ministries care for the whole person and her surrounding society.

5. Programs that develop informal, relaxed friendships with non-Christians. Every ministry described in *Cup of Water, Bread of Life* has arranged for relaxed, "non-churchy" settings where committed Christians with an evangelistic heart can develop informal friendships with non-Christians. These friendships dare not be phony. That is why social ministries that demonstrate practical concern for the whole person are so powerful. Most Christians have few close, ongoing friendships with non-Christians. Growing churches like the ones I studied have corrected that mistake.

6. Relocation among the needy. Years ago, John Perkins taught us the importance of the three Rs for holistic mission (see *A Quiet Revolution*, 1976). The first step, he still insists, is that some people must relocate to the community of need. Vinay and Colleen Samuel moved to the slums of Lingarajapuram just outside India's great city of Bangalore. Australian businessman David Bussau and his family moved to an isolated, devastated village in Bali. The leaders of dynamic urban programs like Rock/Circle and Lawndale in Chicago moved to the inner city. Without that costly obedience, their ministries simply would not have happened.

7. Partnership with the larger body of Christ. But not everybody needs to relocate. All of the stories, in one way or another, involve partnerships between churches with abundant material and technical resources and churches with less. The partnership must be one of mutual dignity, learning, and respect. Financially "poor" churches have much to teach "rich" churches. At the same time, ministries in places like Lawndale, Lingarajapuram, and Bali need outside financial help. If given in a spirit of loving partnership and mutual learning, financial sharing targeted toward nurturing local economic self-sufficiency is essential.

8. The presence of the Holy Spirit. Nothing significant happens without pervasive, long-term commitment to prayer and dependence on the Holy Spirit. Some of the ministries I explored are explicitly charismatic; some are not. But a profound sense of reliance on God the Father, Son, and Holy Spirit flows through all of them.

I am convinced that these principles will work everywhere. The leaders of the superb ministries described in *Cup of Water, Bread of Life* are not superheroes. They are Christians like you and me who have learned key biblical principles. I am certain God stands ready to accomplish powerful things through any church that dares to apply these eight principles in their community.

Injustice Against Women*

An estimate from the United Nations in 1980 stated, "Women work two-thirds of the world's working hours, produce half of the world's food, and yet earn only 10 percent of the world's income and own less than 1 percent of the world's property." Unfortunately, we do not have nearly enough hard data to describe with precision exactly where and how much injustice against women exists today, but we do have enough information to know that blatant injustice against women is widespread.

Missing women. Nobel Laureate Amartya Sen has estimated that approximately one hundred million women are missing. The reason? A cultural preference for boys that leads to neglect of female babies and abortion of female fetuses. All things being equal, the normal gender ratio is about 105 females to every 100 males. However, after ultrasound devices to determine the sex of the fetus became available in the 1970s, the percentage of baby boys at birth jumped dramatically in countries such as China, India, and South Korea. In 1997 in China, for example, 117 male births were recorded for every 100 female births.

* This is a summary of a paper Ron Sider presented on November 15, 2006, at the annual meeting of the Evangelical Theological Society and is now published as "Gender and Justice Today," *Pricilla Papers*, vol. 21, no. 2 [Spring 2007]:4-8.

Unequal education. In most of the developing world, women have less access to education and are more likely to be illiterate than men. In low-income countries in 2001, 46 percent of women could not read, compared to 28 percent of men. The youth (ages 15-24) illiteracy rates provide another measure. For low-income countries in 2001, 31 percent of female youth were illiterate, compared to 19 percent of male youth. In our global information society, where education and knowledge equal power and wealth, inequality in education means injustice.

Unequal health. Michael Todaro, author of one of the most influential texts on economic development, says that women and children are more likely to be malnourished than men. In Latin America, 31 percent of girls are underweight while only 17 percent of boys are. In India, he notes, girls are four times as likely to suffer acute malnutrition as boys; boys are 40 times more likely than girls to be taken to the hospital when ill.

Unequal property ownership/work. The data is far from complete, but women clearly have legal title to vastly less property than do men. In Brazil in 2000, women owned 11 percent of the land and men owned 89 percent. In Mexico in 2003, women owned 22 percent and men 78 percent. And it is generally thought that land ownership is more equal in Latin America than in other developing areas.

The United Nations' Human Development Report 2005 reported that in a large majority of cases, women work more than men. On average, in urban areas, women worked 481 minutes a day and men only 453 in 2005. In rural areas, women worked 617 minutes to men's 515. The vast majority of developed countries reported the same pattern: 423 minutes for women and 403 for men.

Violence against women. On October 7, 2006, the prestigious British medical journal the *Lancet* published the results of a massive World Health Organization study of physical and sexual abuse of women by intimate partners. Interviewing 24,097 women in eleven countries, they found that huge numbers of women in most countries reported experiencing physical violence at least once in their life. The following statistics are representative: 40 percent in Bangladesh; 30 percent in Brazil; 49 percent in Ethiopia; 49 percent in Peru's cities and 61 percent in its rural areas. Astonishing numbers reported physical abuse in just the previous twelve months.

Sexual trafficking/prostitution. The U.S. Department of State estimated on June 5, 2006, that of the 600,000 to 800,000 people trafficked across international borders every year, 80 percent are women and girls. Most of them end up in prostitution. These figures do not include the millions of girls and women that the State Department believes are trafficked within their own national borders every year.

We know enough to realize that all around the world today, men inflict widespread injustice and violence on women. This behavior stands in blatant defiance of the biblical teaching that every person, both male and female, is made in the very image of God and therefore is inestimably precious in the eyes of God. How can we men continue to violate the dignity and equality of women when we remember that our Lord and Savior died for these very women and invites each of them to accept his love and live eternally with him?

In spite of frequent, indeed widespread, failure, Christian faith over the centuries has been a powerful force creating dignity and justice for women. But the task is far from finished. It is time for Christian men around the world to say, "Enough injustice and violence against our sisters!"

One man who is making a difference is Gary Haugen of the International Justice Mission (see www.ijm.org). He works courageously to free enslaved women. Lee Grady, editor of *Charisma* magazine and author of *10 Lies the Church Tells*

Women, focuses much of his work on empowering women in ministry (see www.themordecaiproject.com). I pray that more Christian men will open their hearts to their sisters' suffering and create a contemporary tidal wave that washes away all injustice against women.

Part 5

EVANGELICALISM

Why Would Anyone Ever Want to Be an Evangelical?

I had a tough sell one Saturday morning in 1994 when I was speaking at Colorado College, a secular school in Colorado Springs with a sizeable New Age population. It was the last day of their weeklong lecture series on spirituality. A vast variety of speakers, including one who offered an introduction to yoga, preceded me. I was the token evangelical, and I was there to argue that full-blooded historic Christianity is just what our troubled world needs. The following is a short summary of what I said. I wish I could say they flocked to the front to accept Christ. They didn't. But they did listen carefully.

Evangelicals? Aren't they the folks who bring us TV evangelists with their sex scandals? Aren't all evangelicals right-wing fanatics and gun-toting NRA members who fight all sensible gun control? Aren't evangelicals all a bunch of anti-feminist reactionaries who want women in the kitchen, submissive, barefoot, and pregnant? Don't they want to take away the civil rights of gay Americans? And aren't they intellectual obscurantists who reject modern science? Don't they destroy the environment because they think the world is going to end at any moment, so we might as well use all we can before God blows it to bits?

We all know the stereotypes, and there are *some* who may fit some of those stereotypes. But many evangelicals do not. I am an evangelical Christian, and I don't fit that image. Many evangelicals, in fact, believe it is precisely historic, biblical Christianity that provides the best basis for our support for human rights, our care for the environment, the equality of women, and whole, healthy families.

Evangelical Christians think many modern thinkers have committed intellectual suicide. Modern folk claim people, indeed all living things, are merely the product of a blind, materialistic process governed by chance.

Notice what follows if they are right. If everything results from matter and chance, then truth and ethics do not exist. People are simply sophisticated materialistic machines. Ethical values are totally subjective, merely an expression of our individual feelings. As the famous philosopher and mathematician Bertrand Russell said, those who have the best poison gas will determine the ethics of the future.

Christians have a radically *different* view of the world. We believe all life is the creation of a loving, personal God. Human beings are free, responsible persons whose deepest joy and ultimate obligation is to live in right relationship with their loving Creator. Created in God's image, every human being has ultimate value. Ethical values are therefore an expression of the very nature of God, not merely the relativistic, arbitrary product of a blind, materialistic process.

Jesus taught and lived a radical ethic that deeply challenged the status quo. That alone might have been enough to get him put away, but Jesus also did something more. He made outrageous, even blasphemous, claims about himself. He claimed divine authority to forgive sins. At his trial, he acknowledged he was the Son of God.

Jesus was crucified for two reasons. First, because he was a dangerous social radical. Second, because they said he was a blasphemer who claimed to be the only Son of God. If Jesus' death were the end of the story, then our faith is in vain and we Christians are, as St. Paul said, of all people most to be pitied. But if it is true, as Christians believe, that this is not the end of the story—that Jesus Christ did, indeed, rise from the dead—then that confirms his astonishing claims and offers a reason for modern folk to explore biblical faith.

Is there any solid evidence that this carpenter from Nazareth was really alive on the third day? I have examined the historical evidence carefully. As a historian, I find the evidence surprisingly strong. The most objective, unbiased historical conclusion is that Jesus was probably alive on the third day.

How could that happen? Even with all our modern technology, we cannot do such a thing. The first Christians said God raised Jesus from the dead. That seems to be the most reasonable explanation. Jesus' resurrection strongly suggests that the Christian view of the world, not the modern secular one, is true.

The biblical, evangelical Christianity I am describing works out concretely in the tough issues of our time. For example, our ravaged environment and our devastated families.

Our Environmental Crisis

The crisis is real and urgent. New Age folk like Shirley MacLaine say the solution is monism, which teaches that all is divine.

But notice what this view implies. First of all, if monism is right and all is divine, then all is good, and we cannot even distinguish between good and evil. Furthermore, the ideal in eastern monism is to escape this material world, to turn within, and to merge with the all. The material world is an illusion, and the ideal is to merge with the Divine All in the way a drop of water falls into the ocean and disappears. The person loses all individual identity.

How does such a worldview offer a solution to our environmental crisis? If the material world is an illusion, why worry about it?

Biblical faith is radically different. It teaches that you and I and all the world around us, though very important, are not divine. We are the creation of an all-powerful, all-loving Creator. We are finite but good. The material world is so good that the God of the universe, the Creator of the galaxies, became flesh. The material world is so good that Jesus Christ rose *bodily* from death. The material world is so good that Jesus Christ promises to return to this earth and complete the victory over injustice, evil, and death itself.

Some environmentalists say persons are no more important than monkeys or moles or mushrooms. To claim a special status for people, they say, is "speciesism." If that is true, then civilization collapses. We have no right to use or even eat *anything* in the world around us. Nor is re-divinizing the material world the answer.

The biblical view is more carefully balanced. Persons alone are created in the image of God, and persons have the special task of being God's stewards over the rest of creation on this planet. The Genesis story says people are to "care for" God's garden; the word literally means we are to *serve* it.

The Bible also says the nonhuman creation has independent worth and significance entirely apart from you and me. The heavens declare the glory of God. The sun, moon, and stars sing praises to their Creator. The Creator cares about every endangered species. We should too.

Christians have often neglected this full biblical teaching on the creation. And we have, along with Enlightenment naturalists, helped destroy the environment. For that, I repent. But if we are faithful to biblical teaching, we have a far better foundation for lovingly caring for this gorgeous creation than does eastern monism or goddess worship.

Families and Feminism

Everybody knows the American family is a disaster area.

Social scientists regularly report the sad effects of divorce and broken families. Our society also experiences incredible levels of rape, incest, and all kinds of sexual and physical violence against women.

The answer is not some kind of conservative religious patriarchy in which the husband dominates the home, ruling wife and children as lord and master. In fact, that kind of patriarchy probably *contributes* to sexual abuse in the home. But neither is the solution the kind of radical feminism that rejects marriage and places personal self-fulfillment above responsibility to children.

Here again, biblical faith is just what we need. Jesus Christ was a feminist. He treated women as equals, challenging the patriarchal attitudes of his day. The over-arching principle St. Paul spells out for husbands and wives in Ephesians 5 is *mutual submission*. Jesus calls men and women to sexual purity and to joyful, life-long marriage covenant.

Let me put it personally. My wife, Arbutus, and I have been married for thirty-two years. We believe in full mutuality in our marriage. We make our decisions together. We love sex, even in our fifties, and we have always been faithful. There have been times in our marriage when we have struggled and hurt each other. We once spent six months in marriage counseling. But we were and are committed to each other for life, so we worked through those difficulties to a time of even greater joy and love. Our three children have never had to worry that we would get a divorce. We are both feminists, biblical feminists like Jesus, whom we love and worship.

The full biblical view of family, marriage, and the equality of women is what our aching homes need. You cannot have happy marriages if you screw around all through college and are never sure, even after marriage, if your partner will be faithful to you. Your marriage will not last if you see it as a limited contract to dissolve as soon as it does not feel good and fulfill your immediate personal needs. The demand for instant gratification and self-centered individualism are central causes of the hell that rampages through our marriages.

There is a better way. The way Jesus taught. It is possible, and in the long run full of greater joy and fulfillment, to reserve sex for marriage and remain faithful to your spouse. The full biblical view of family and feminism is just what this hurting society needs.

Why would anybody ever want to be an evangelical? Because, I believe, biblical faith is true. And because it works. If you don't believe me, I challenge you to examine the evidence openly and without bias. Then I dare you to try it for yourself.

Are Evangelical Leaders on Their Way to Hell?

There is strong biblical reason for thinking that many evangelical leaders are idolatrous heretics. If that statement seems a bit strong, ask yourself these questions: Do today's evangelical leaders come even close to preaching and teaching about God's concern for the poor the way the Bible does? What does the Bible say about those who neglect the poor and those who fail to teach their people what God tells them to say?

Three sets of facts simply do not fit together: (1) There is widespread poverty in our world. (2) The Bible says God and his faithful people have a special concern for the poor. (3) North American Christians give less and less every year.

In July 2000, the World Bank reported that 1.2 billion people are obliged to try and survive on one dollar a day. Another two billion have only two dollars a day to live on. The richest 20 percent of the world's people (including the vast majority of people in the United States) are 150 times as rich as the poorest 20 percent.

The Bible is full of texts demanding that God's people share God's concern for the poor. In fact, these biblical texts fill almost two hundred pages in the book I edited called *For They Shall Be Fed*. Jesus said bluntly that those who neglect the poor will go to hell: "Depart from me, you who are cursed, into the eternal fire prepared for the devil and his angels. For I was hungry and you gave me nothing to eat" (Matthew 25:41-42 NIV). If Jesus meant what he said, does not the widespread neglect of the poor in the American church mean we are in danger of eternal damnation?

Tragically, every year since 1969, per capita congregational giving in the United States has declined. It is now about a quarter of a tithe. Most of us are substantially more wealthy today than we were thirty years ago. The size of the average new house has almost doubled in the last forty years. We have vastly more material abundance but, inversely, give less to the work of the kingdom. Mammon is winning the battle for most Christian hearts.

Obviously, our Christian leaders—pastors, Sunday school teachers, seminary professors, popular speakers—are guilty of colossal failure. According to the Bible, leaders are placed as "watchmen" over God's people: if leaders issue God's warning and the people ignore it, the people are held responsible. But if the leaders fail to warn the people, then God holds the leaders accountable: "When I say to a wicked man, 'You will surely die,' and you do not warn him or speak out to dissuade him from his evil ways in order to save his life, that wicked man will die for his sin, and I will hold you accountable for his blood" (Ezekiel 3:18 NIV).

Would anybody claim that evangelical leaders today are talking as much about God's concern for the poor as the Bible does? Would anyone deny that this is the second most common theme in the Bible? If evangelical pastors reviewed their sermons, if evangelical congregations reviewed their educational curricula and total congregational spending, if parachurch leaders reviewed their organizations' programs, could they honestly say that seeking to empower the poor is one of their top agenda items?

Is it not heresy to largely ignore the second most common theme in the Bible and then pretend that one is offering biblical Christianity to one's people? If Ezekiel 3 is right, will not God hold evangelical leaders accountable for their widespread failure to teach their people about God's concern for the poor?

Evangelical leaders have four options:

1. The radical option. You can preach fiery sermons and get thrown out. I don't recommend it.

2. The conformist option. Basically, you can preach and teach what the people want to hear, throwing in an occasional word about the poor on World Hunger Sunday.

3. The calculating option. You can resolve to lead your people into greater concern for the poor, so you calculate just how much they can take without getting really upset. You push them, but never to the point of endangering your job. At the end of the day, this is just a more sophisticated version of the conformist option, just a careful assessment of what the market will bear.

4. The Spirit-filled, costly option. You can decide you would rather have Jesus than parsonage or pulpit or presidency. You decide to lovingly, gently, clearly teach all that the Bible says about justice for the poor.

And what will such an option lead to? Embracing a biblical balance of prayer and action, preaching and modeling, evangelism and social ministry, worship and mission will often lead to transformed, growing congregations.

But not always. Sometimes they throw you out. But unless you are ready to risk that, it means that no matter how you rationalize it, no matter how you massage your conscience, you really worship job security more than Jesus.

An Alternative Evangelical Voice

The cover of *Prism* magazine, the journal of Evangelicals for Social Action, an organization I serve as president, bears the phrase "America's Alternative Evangelical Voice." I'm frequently asked, "Alternative to what?"

Mainstream evangelicalism is essentially "conformed to this world." It has lost its passion for costly discipleship. It is far less concerned with the poor, the environment, and the dignity and equality of women and minorities than the Christ revealed in the Bible is. Sometimes the cultural conformity is blatant, sometimes subtle. But it is everywhere. You can see it in our materialism. In our sexual practices and divorce rates. In our unmitigated nationalism. And in our antipathy toward peacemakers.

Is there anybody who would argue that American evangelicals care as much about the poor as Jesus or the prophets? That Jesus' affirmation of the dignity of women is the norm in most evangelical churches? Or that Jesus' call to sexual purity is genuinely obeyed? Or that the Scripture's call to steward creation is a priority?

ESA and *Prism* feel compelled to be loving critics and offer an alternative to mainstream evangelicalism precisely because we believe unconditional submission to Christ and unswerving adherence to biblical truth demand it. That brings me to the second major adjective in our self-description.

In June 1996, I attended a conference devoted to the theme

"Re-Forming the Center." It was the final two-day meeting in a three-year process seeking to rethink the liberal/conservative chasm in American Protestantism. A majority of the organizers and the participants were from evangelical institutions. What astonished me, however, was the draft proposal offering a new center for American Protestantism. The organizers wrote a document proposing a new "fuzzy, post-modernist center" with no boundaries—a center that does not exclude anyone!— as a way forward for American Protestants. Any discussion of the nature of Christ (Christology) was omitted, it was explained, because of all the allegedly contradictory views of Christ over the centuries.

I find such a proposal disturbing. There is increasing evidence that self-identification as an evangelical does not guarantee a commitment to core evangelical beliefs. George Barna has discovered in his surveys that a majority of American Christians who say they are born again do not believe in "absolute truth." Half doubt the reality of a real devil, while three in ten don't believe in Christ's resurrection. And 39 percent suppose that one can earn a place in heaven "if a person is generally good or does enough good things for others during their life."

Apparently the definition of *evangelicalism* is getting pretty fuzzy indeed.

So, what is an evangelical? Historically, the word has been the preferred Protestant self-designation at three major points. In the Reformation, evangelicals stressed the authority of Scripture over church tradition (*sola Scriptura*) and our dependence on grace over our own good works (*sola gratia*). The only basis for standing before our holy God is trust in Christ's death for us on the cross.

In the eighteenth and nineteenth centuries, the evangelical revivals of the Great Awakenings challenged "dead orthodoxy" (*just* believing the right things) with a ringing call to a personal, living encounter with Christ, a passion to share his gospel, and a call for social engagement. The struggle against slavery, for worker's rights, and early feminism were all rooted in the evangelical revivals in England and America.

At the beginning of the twentieth century, when liberal theologians denied the uniqueness, deity, and resurrection of Christ and abandoned the authority of the Scriptures, Christians concerned for the fundamentals insisted that the central theological doctrines of historic Christian orthodoxy are indispensable.

ESA is evangelical because it seeks to stand on that solid theological foundation articulated at those three historic moments by people who called themselves evangelical. ESA talks about the scandal of the evangelical social conscience and its cultural conformity, but we also insist that God's authoritative Word demands *both* ortho-praxis and orthodoxy, and that faithful living and biblical theology depend on each other. In fact, it is only because we believe that the carpenter from Nazareth is "true God and true man"—our risen Savior—that we seek to imitate his astounding concern for the poor and marginalized. We emphasize evangelism and social engagement by the power of the Spirit because Jesus' gospel of the kingdom demands it. We insist on a balanced biblical social agenda— both family values and peacemaking, both respect for life and concern for the poor, both sexual integrity and care for creation—precisely because the Bible reveals a God who cares about all those things.

Gently, insistently, *Prism* tries to prod Christians to reject a watered-down, distorted, comfortable Savior and to surrender instead to the Jesus of the Bible.

That is why we call ourselves an *alternative* evangelical voice.

Needed: A Progressive Evangelical Network

We urgently need an effective, progressive evangelical network.

At precisely the moment when American society as a whole is beginning to search urgently for deeper spiritual foundations, most Americans identify evangelicalism with a right-wing minority that is perceived as strident and reactionary. Many Americans think evangelicals want to deny the equality of women, care little about the environment, blame the poor for their plight, trample the civil rights of gays, abandon the struggle to overcome racism, and abolish the separation of church and state. Not surprisingly, many Americans think evangelicals have nothing positive to offer our national politics, just division and hatred.

But we at Evangelicals for Social Action believe a holistic, evangelical approach is just what our society needs. Our society needs people who will work to restore the family yet not reinstate patriarchy; who affirm biblical sexual standards yet respect the civil rights of homosexuals; who care for and struggle to protect creation, the unborn, and the poor; who want greater openness to religious expression in public life without excluding those who do not share their faith; who understand that the solution to our desperate urban problems is ultimately spiritual and yet still acknowledge that change must be structural as well as personal; and who want to expand nongovernmental solutions to poverty without abandoning the government's obligation to care for and empower the poor.

There has always been a strong, progressive evangelical voice within North American evangelicalism. Evangelicals like evangelist Charles Finney—the Billy Graham of the early nineteenth century—were key leaders in the great crusade against slavery. Early feminism was rooted in the same progressive evangelical tradition.

Nor have progressive evangelicals disappeared. Just look around at the massive work that evangelicals are doing today. Evangelical relief and development agencies raise hundreds of millions of dollars each year to empower the poor. InterVarsity Christian Fellowship, the largest Christian university movement, combines evangelistic outreach with a strong discipling program that often includes social engagement. Tony Campolo leads holistic evangelistic campaigns and stirs up people everywhere with his Spirit-blessed, fiery oratory, urging people to combine evangelism and social concern. John Perkins's Christian Community Development Association now represents several hundred holistic programs among the poor, combining evangelism and community development. Christians for Biblical Equality works to make sure their affirmation of biblical feminism is not a white middle-class concern that neglects the poor and marginalized. Habitat for Humanity is well on its way to becoming the largest house builder in the world. Richard Foster's Renovare works for the renewal of the church in a way that at once rekindles the fires of contemplative disciplines and still embraces social justice.

In short, a vast array of progressive evangelical programs are already out there getting the job done at the grass roots. The Religious Right simply does not speak for the majority of evangelical Christians. But somehow, we have allowed others to seize the microphone and persuade the media that the leaders of the Right speak for all of us. This must change.

How can we change? What do we need? What don't we need?

First, we do not need a progressive version of the Religious Right. Nor do we need one organization that tries to take over other organizations. The last thing the church, or this country, needs is another power-hungry religious organization.

We need a new fellowship that encourages existing ministries to pray, dream, and plan together in a way that maximizes the other's potential and contribution. We need to encourage progressive evangelical leaders to meet together once a year for a couple of days to pray and dream and discuss new cooperative efforts. We need to let organizations with mutually supportive visions cooperate better and serve each other more effectively. For too long we have competed for scarce resources and built our own kingdoms rather than working for the glory of *the* kingdom.

We must become more effective popularizers and communicators. We need to effectively summon Christians to costly discipleship and help Christians integrate evangelism, social transformation, and spiritual formation in ways that are relevant and engaging. We need progressive evangelicals on TV and radio, opening the Scriptures and declaring its whole message. We need to take seriously the challenge of Christian media and not abandon it to one-sided voices that care more for ratings than for the whole person.

We need a new kind of evangelistic crusade that understands the necessity of evangelism and social concern. We need to call people to a discipleship that is more than a fire escape. We need new programs to come alongside local congregations and offer concrete, practical help so they can truly integrate evangelism and social ministry. Churches want to do that. They need help.

Nor dare we neglect public policy. Politics is not all-important, but it can make a crucial difference. Too often, we have rushed into the public square without doing our homework. We need sophisticated social analyses solidly grounded in biblical principles. And we need structures to translate that thinking into political effectiveness.

We don't need a new movement of progressive evangelicals. It's already happening. All over the country, people are doing the creative, exciting work of the kingdom. What we need is a way to more effectively link and serve those Christians, churches, and Christian missions that are living out the real thing.

ESA plays this role in many ways, but we want to be partners in a larger progressive evangelical network. We want to encourage and serve others who share the same vision. As we work at that larger partnership, ESA is grateful that God keeps opening doors to do more. We want to band together and let the world see not the narrow, politicized version but the whole gospel of Christ that it so urgently needs.

On Giants' Shoulders

Many Christians hardly know the name Carl F. H. Henry. They should. After Billy Graham, Henry is probably the most influential American evangelical leader in the second half of the twentieth century.

To appreciate his enormous contribution, we need to understand the dismal situation of American evangelicalism in the 1940s. After decades-long warfare between fundamentalists and liberal social-gospelers, theologically conservative Christians were marginalized, inward looking, divided, antiintellectual, and largely disengaged from public life and culture in general. Many embraced a dispensationalism preoccupied with detailed speculation (and quarrels) about Christ's second coming. Non-evangelicals dominated theological education and mainline denominations. Evangelicals had few good scholars or strong colleges and were little concerned for society's social problems.

A small circle of creative young evangelical pioneers in the 1940s developed a broader biblical vision and launched a cluster of initiatives that revolutionized American fundamentalism, indeed American Christianity, over the next fifty years.

Henry's groundbreaking little book *The Uneasy Conscience of Modern Fundamentalism* (1947) laid out the vision. He pled with theological conservatives (then called fundamentalists) to focus on central biblical doctrines of historic Christian orthodoxy rather than to fight over minor disagreements; to turn away from their neglect of solid scholarship, lack of concern for social problems, and separatist withdrawal; to understand that sin is both personal and social; and to dare to think through a solidly biblical theology and Christian worldview that would engage every area of culture with an orthodox Christian alternative to surrounding theological liberalism and secularism.

It took decades of hard struggle, but they succeeded. This small circle of friends founded Fuller Seminary to renew serious evangelical theological scholarship. Today evangelicals dominate theological education; almost all the large seminaries are evangelical. They began *Christianity Today* magazine to counter the liberal *Christian Century*. Today *Christianity Today*'s circulation and influence are vastly greater than the *Christian Century*'s. They established a cluster of evangelical youth movements, including InterVarsity Christian Fellowship, Young Life, and Youth for Christ. Today all the large Christian high school and university movements are evangelical. They promoted rigorous evangelical scholarship. Today there are thousands of excellent evangelical scholars teaching in secular universities and the nearly one hundred evangelical colleges and universities. Mainline denominations have declined dramatically. Almost all growing Protestant congregations are evangelical (whether Pentecostal/charismatic or not). Today most evangelical leaders agree that social action (including political engagement) is an important part (along with evangelism) of biblical obedience.

Serious problems remain, of course, but by any reckoning this was a stunning achievement. Out of a marginalized, privatized fundamentalism at mid-century has emerged a vigorous, broad evangelical movement that clearly represents the dominant voice in American Protestantism. Evangelical Christianity is growing rapidly and becoming more holistic in most parts of the globe.

In spite of all its faults, I believe evangelical Protestantism remains the most faithful broad Christian movement today. For that we owe a huge debt to that little circle of gifted pioneers led by Billy Graham and Carl Henry, who half a century ago dared to dream boldly and innovate courageously out of passionate devotion to the biblical Christ. They were giants who have brought us to this time of glorious opportunity.

Only decades from now will future historians discover whether this and the next generation manage to transcend the limitations that, alas, hindered even these excellent leaders. But if we do come to see more clearly, by God's grace, it will be because we stand on the shoulders of these twentieth-century evangelical giants.

Recommended books by Carl F. H. Henry: *God, Revelation, and Authority; Toward a Recovery of Christian Belief: The Rutherford Lectures; Twilight of a Great Civilization: The Drift Toward Neo-Paganism; Aspects of Christian Social Ethics; The Identity of Jesus of Nazareth.*

What Should Evangelicals Do Now?

The world abruptly changed on September 11, 2001. Should the events of that day bring about the kind of profound cultural shift that occurred in the 1960s, evangelicals are far better equipped to respond now than we were then.

In the '60s we were ready neither to embrace what was right (racial and economic justice, the dignity and equality of women) nor to critique what was wrong (perverse sexual and family values, moral relativism). In the four decades since, we have seen a scholarly resurgence that has given us literally thousands of brilliant evangelical scholars. We have made great progress in combining evangelism and social action and have made significant strides in empowering the poor and understanding economic justice. We have even begun, however late, to work seriously at racial reconciliation. If we can muster the right combination of confidence and compassion, evangelicals might in the next twenty years write a glorious chapter in the history of biblical Christianity.

Four things are required to accomplish this. First, we must lead with compassionate service. Second, we must discover a winsome way to invite our hurting neighbors to come home to Christ and biblical values. Third, we must embrace a global perspective. Finally, we must develop a widely endorsed evangelical vision for shaping culture and public life.

Imagine a world in which the first image that pops into secular minds at the mention of the word *evangelical* is "compassionate service." Think of the impact Christianity would have if Christians were better known for caring for AIDS sufferers than for condemning homosexuals; better known for demonstrating committed marriages of mutuality and joy than for denouncing out-of-wedlock births; better known for championing economic opportunity for the poor than for advocating tax cuts for the wealthy.

Second, we need to be winsome in our witness. Jesus is what our hurting society needs, and biblical truth is what our confused postmodernist neighbors long for, however unwittingly. But they will never hear the message if the messenger repulses them. Evangelicals are often right in their condemnation of contemporary morals but so stringent and unloving in their approach that unbelievers turn away in disgust. Evangelical philosopher Nicholas Wolterstorff, a professor at Yale, tells how every year he has a few evangelical students who attack secular ideas with vigorous harshness and how he has to take them aside, explain that he essentially agrees with them, and then urge them to strive for a gentler tone. Let us be known more for what we affirm than for what we reject, more for what we love than for what we hate.

Third, evangelicals should be leaders in a global vision. We have led the way in spreading the gospel all around the globe, and we have developed vast relief and development agencies to work with the poor in every continent. We know that "white western" Christians are now a minority in the one worldwide body of Christ. Now is the time to understand and live out two distinct truths: first, that every living human being is our neighbor, a member of the Creator's one human family; and second, that our commitment to the one worldwide body of believing Christians transcends all national or ethnic loyalties.

Finally, evangelicals desperately need a coherent, widely accepted cultural and political vision. Because our public engagement is confused, contradictory, and disorganized, American evangelicals are squandering a historic opportunity to shape the culture and political life of this nation. Evangelicals make up one-quarter of all voters, but our political influence is small and spasmodic. We lack the kind of coherent vision that papal encyclicals and bishops' documents offer Catholics.

It is urgent that evangelicals engage in a careful process that draws on the best skills of our scholars and the experience of our activists from a full range of traditions and perspectives. We must stop working at cross-purposes and instead transcend what Ed Dobson, for years Jerry Falwell's vice president at Moral Majority, so aptly called the non-strategy of "ready, fire, aim." If this generation of evangelicals is to have any lasting cultural and political impact, it must articulate a biblically grounded, sophisticated political framework that a wide range of diverse evangelical gatekeepers endorses and works together to implement.

That framework, if it reflects a biblical balance, will be pro-life and pro-poor, pro-racial justice and pro-family, pro-environment and pro-sexual integrity. This kind of "consistently pro-life" agenda is at the heart of current Catholic social thought, and if evangelicals can develop and embrace a coherent and biblically balanced vision of our own, we will be ready to develop a strong, sustained cooperation with Catholics to shape culture and politics. If evangelicals and Catholics—together representing 50 percent of all American voters—were to sustain such a partnership over a twenty-year period, we could transform American public life.

While the post-September 11 world is frightening, I see more opportunity than danger for evangelicals—but only if compassionate service becomes our trademark, winsome gentleness characterizes our witness, global vision replaces self-centered nationalism, and a coherent and biblically balanced cultural and political vision emerges to guide our public engagement.

A New Evangelical Consensus on Politics?

I'm truly excited and grateful to God for what might just be a historic document that significantly shapes evangelical political engagement in the next decade.

On October 7, 2004, the board of directors of the National Association of Evangelicals (NAE) unanimously adopted "For the Health of the Nation: An Evangelical Call to Civic Responsibility" as its official policy statement for its work on public policy. I'm hardly a neutral observer (since I co-chaired the process that produced the declaration), but I think the document is strong, biblically balanced, and potentially very significant.

The NAE is the largest association of American evangelicals. It has twenty-five million members in over fifty denominations in forty-five thousand congregations. If even a large minority of those people started lobbying and voting on the basis of this document, American politics would change.

For many years, I have been critical of a great deal of evangelical political activity. Lacking a biblical balance of concern for all that the Bible says God cares about, it has often been narrowly focused on just a couple of issues, such as abortion and family. It has largely lacked any deep conceptual foundations in a carefully constructed political philosophy like that developed for Catholics in a century of papal encyclicals.

I used to dream about the unlikely possibility that a group of evangelical leaders, representing everyone from Jim Wallis to James Dobson, would engage in a process to develop a common set of principles for political engagement—in short, the beginnings of an evangelical political philosophy. I even proposed the idea in a few speeches and a chapter in a book. But the whole idea seemed highly unlikely.

Well, it has happened!

Between 2002 and 2004, Diane Knippers, president of the conservative Institute on Religion and Democracy, and I have co-chaired a process authorized by the NAE to develop just that kind of consensus document for evangelicals. Over fifteen scholars wrote preparatory papers on key issues, and these were published in a book edited by Knippers and myself called *Toward an Evangelical Public Policy: Political Strategies for the Health of the Nation.* A drafting committee, led by David Neff (editor of *Christianity Today*), produced an initial draft from these papers and then revised the document many times in response to suggestions from numerous people. A wide range of evangelical leaders were invited to add their signatures to the final draft approved by the NAE.

Why is "For the Health of the Nation" so potentially important? Primarily because what it says is now the official platform of twenty-five million evangelicals, and it says several important things that many evangelicals have not said or practiced. I underline four here.

First, the declaration clearly—and repeatedly!—adopts what ESA folk often summarize as a "pro-poor *and* pro-life, pro-racial justice *and* pro-family" approach: "The Bible makes it clear that God cares a great deal about the well-being of marriage, the family, the sanctity of human life, justice for the poor, care for creation, peace, freedom, and racial justice. While individual persons and organizations are at times called by God to concentrate on one or two issues, faithful evangelical civic engagement must champion a biblically balanced agenda."

Second, the declaration clearly affirms the importance of transforming both individuals and institutions. Even as evangelicals became much more politically engaged in the last two decades, researchers (for example, Chris Smith) discovered that evangelicals still continued to think that the primary way to change society is "one person at a time" through personal conversion. This declaration reaffirms the importance of personal conversion in producing social change. But it lays equal emphasis on structural change: "Christian civic engagement must seek to transform both individuals and institutions. . . . Lasting social change requires both personal conversion and institutional renewal and reform."

Third, the declaration clearly calls for humility and civility in our political activity and insists that our commitment to other brothers and sisters in the one body of Christ far transcends any ongoing political disagreements: "We must be clear that biblical faith is vastly larger and richer than every limited, inevitably imperfect political agenda, and that commitment to the Lordship of Christ and his one body far transcends all political commitments."

Fourth, the declaration clearly rejects excessive nationalism: "We confess that our primary allegiance is to Christ, his kingdom, and Christ's worldwide body of believers, not to any nation. . . . As Christian citizens of the U.S., we must keep our eyes open to the potentially self-destructive tendencies of our society and our government. We must also balance our natural affection for our country with a love for people of all nations."

I could go on. But read it for yourself on the NAE website (www.nae.net). Consider studying it in a Sunday school class or small group. Most important, pray that the evangelical world will not only endorse but actually implement this declaration. One-quarter of all U.S. voters are evangelicals. Think of the impact if half of them started lobbying and voting on the basis of this "biblically balanced agenda."

Just a dream? Some dreams come true. Join me in praying that this hope becomes reality.

The Scandal of the Evangelical Conscience

My friend Graham Cyster, an evangelical church leader in South Africa during the struggle against apartheid, was once smuggled into an underground Communist cell. "Tell us about the gospel of Jesus Christ," they said. So Graham talked about the way reconciliation with God leads to a reconciled body of Christ, where there is neither Jew nor Greek, black nor white. When he'd finished, a seventeen-year-old boy who had been listening intently said, "That is wonderful. Show me where I can see that happening."

My friend's face fell. He admitted sadly that he did not know of any good example in South Africa. "Then the whole thing is a piece of [expletive]," the young man yelled. Within a month the youth left the country to join the military wing of the anti-apartheid movement.

That experience led Graham to resolve never again to preach what he was not trying to live.

One of the greatest scandals today—at least as devastating as the "scandal of the evangelical mind" bemoaned by Wheaton College historian Mark Noll—is that vast numbers of evangelicals do not practice what they preach. The polling data is clear. "Gallup and Barna hand us survey after survey," evangelical theologian Michael Horton says, "demonstrating that evangelical Christians are likely to embrace lifestyles every bit as hedonistic, materialistic, self-centered, and sexually immoral as the world in general." One wonders if the central evangelical belief—in a new birth through personal faith in Christ, who sends the Holy Spirit to transform us into the very image of Christ—is in reality a farce, a fraud, or a false promise.

George Gallup Jr. speaks of an "ethics gap—the difference between the way people think of themselves and the way they actually are." The following statistics—taken from polls prior to 2004 by Barna, Gallup, Green, Ronsvalles, and Smith—are disturbing:

- Only 8 percent of those who identified themselves as "born-again" Christians tithe—that is, give 10 percent of their earnings to the work of the church/charity. (Barna, 1999)
- The more money Christians make, the less likely they are to tithe: 89 percent of those making less than 20,000 dollars a year tithe, while 4 percent of those making 40,000 to 59,000 tithe, and only 1 percent of those making 75,000 to 99,000 tithe. (Barna, 1999)
- General giving of Christians to their churches declined as a percentage of income from 3.14 percent in 1968 to 2.48 percent in 1994. And evangelical giving, which had been dramatically greater than that of other Christians, crept closer and closer to the average. (Ronsvalles)
- In the early 1990s, when the average church member gave twenty dollars a year for global outreach (evangelism and social ministry), the average American church member spent 164 dollars on soft drinks and over a thousand dollars on recreation—while over one billion people tried to survive on one dollar a day. (Ronsvalles)
- Seventy-seven percent of evangelicals say that volunteering in local community organizations is "very important," but only 32 percent actually volunteer "a lot." (Smith)
- The percentage of "born-again" Christians who have experienced divorce is higher than that of non-Christians: 26 percent versus 22 percent. (Barna, 1999)

- Twenty-five percent of "born-again" Christians have lived with a member of the opposite sex without getting married. (Barna, 2001)
- Born-again adults spend 700 percent more time per week watching television than participating in an activity such as prayer, Bible reading, and worship. (Barna, 2000)
- Evangelicals are more likely than Catholics or mainline Christians to object to having an African-American neighbor. (Gallup, 1989)
- Twenty-six percent of the "high-commitment" evangelicals and 46 percent of the "lower commitment" evangelicals think premarital sex is acceptable. (Green, 2001)
- Thirteen percent of "high-commitment" evangelicals even think it is acceptable for married persons to have extramarital sex. (Green, 2001)

Whether the issue is marriage and sexuality or money and care for the poor, evangelicals today are living scandalously unbiblical lives. Large numbers of evangelicals live in flat contradiction to biblical norms. Our lifestyles contradict our theology and undermine our witness.

Think of the witness we would have for Christ if virtually every time non-Christians met evangelicals they discovered joyful people in committed marriages, leaders in overcoming racism, and generous partners in empowering the poor.

Instead we have been seduced by society's individualistic, adulterous, materialistic values. We have neglected our fundamental belief that a living personal relationship with Jesus Christ produces marvelous, lifelong conversion. What an irony that while evangelicals loudly support governmental faith-based initiatives (based on the assumption that spiritual faith can transform broken people), the polling data suggest that in many crucial areas evangelicals are not living any differently from their unbelieving neighbors.

Unfaithful evangelical lifestyles are a blatant denial of

Jesus' gospel. If the gospel were merely the forgiveness of sins, we could accept the gospel and go on living in the same racist, adulterous, materialistic way. But if the gospel is the good news of Christ's kingdom, as Jesus taught, and if part of the good news is that right now a new redeemed community of transformed persons living in the power of the Holy Spirit is breaking into history, then whenever so-called Christians live as the world does, their very lives are evidence against Jesus' teaching.

We need to recover the biblical truth that God is blazing holiness as well as overwhelming love. We need to recover the biblical teaching on the awfulness of sin and the necessity of repentance and sanctification. We need to turn away from American individualism and recover the New Testament understanding of mutual accountability. We need to bring all our people into small discipleship groups of genuine accountability so we can, as John Wesley said, "watch over one another in love." We need to rediscover the almost totally neglected biblical teaching on church discipline.

The scandal of the evangelical conscience today mocks our evangelistic efforts and breaks the heart of our Savior. If we will not repent and change, we should admit that the whole thing is a fraud.

Never Before in American History

Something historic happened March 28-31, 2006, in Atlanta. For the first time ever in American history, official representatives of major denominations from all five family traditions agreed formally to launch a new ecumenical organization called Christian Churches Together in the USA.

What is so new and important is that the Roman Catholic Church and evangelical/Pentecostal denominations are fully engaged. These two families had not joined earlier ecumenical efforts that included mainline Protestants, the Orthodox, and African-American denominations. Now all five families have decided to work together in CCT.

CCT's purpose is to help the various Christian theological traditions understand each other better through common prayer and honest dialogue and then to witness together to society through faithful evangelism and the shaping of public life. An annual three-day meeting of leaders of denominations and national Christian organizations will be the primary initial vehicle for dialogue and decision making.

CCT has a solidly orthodox christological and trinitarian theological foundation. Our common confession is that Jesus Christ is God and Savior in accordance with the Scriptures and that we worship one God—Father, Son, and Holy Spirit.

I have had the privilege of being at all preparatory meetings, starting in 2001. From the first meeting, there was consensus that it was time to establish a new, much broader table of ecumenical conversation and cooperation. It was not clear at the beginning whether a critical mass of evangelical and Pentecostal denominations would join, but several of us evangelical and Pentecostal participants worked vigorously to encourage our family's participation. The result is that eight of the founding denominations of CCT come from the evangelical/Pentecostal family: Christian Reformed, Church of God (Cleveland), Open Bible Churches, International Pentecostal Holiness Church, Salvation Army, Free Methodist Church, Evangelical Covenant Church, and Church of God of Prophecy.

According to CCT bylaws, 80 percent of the participants/members must be national denominations; no more than 20 percent may be national Christian organizations. Evangelicals for Social Action is privileged to be a founding member in this latter category, as is World Vision.

One significant early decision that made it easier for evangelicals/Pentecostals to join was the choice to require that all decision making in CCT be by consensus. That prevents a bare majority from ignoring the views of the minority.

CCT would have been ready to launch at the June 2005 meeting except for the fact that we did not yet have any African-American denominations on board. Given the tragic history of slavery and racism in this nation, we felt we must wait until African-American denominations had joined. Fortunately, two black national Baptist conventions (including the largest, led by Dr. William Shaw) have now become founding members. AMEN, the largest evangelical Latino organization in the States, is also a founding member.

The press release of the Atlanta meeting quoted a lament about the brokenness of the body of Christ from the first meeting in 2001. It conveys powerfully the impetus for CCT:

> We lament that we are divided and that our divisions
> too often result in distrust, misunderstanding, fear, and

even hostility among us. We long for the broken body of
Christ to be made whole, where unity can be celebrated
in the midst of our diversity. We long for more common
witness, vision, and mission.

From the beginning, we were clear in CCT that our first
tasks were to pray, worship, and dialogue together in order
to better understand each other. But we also looked forward
to the time when we could witness together.

Each year for several annual meetings, we have spent
time on three things: worship and fellowship; business; and
discussion of a major theme. In Atlanta, the major issue was
overcoming domestic poverty. CCT is clear that (a) this is just
one of many issues we will discuss; and (b) that CCT will not
become an anti-poverty organization.

However, we did find strong consensus in Atlanta that "a
commitment to overcome poverty is central to the mission of
the church and essential to our unity in Christ." Therefore we
agreed that CCT would develop a strategy to use the unique
gifts and influence of the key church leaders in CCT to summon both our churches and the nation to confront the reality
of widespread poverty in the richest nation in history.

I think CCT represents a truly historic development in
American church history. Already the thirty-four denominations and national Christian organizations that have joined
represent more than one hundred million American Christians. CCT is the broadest, and largest, fellowship of Christian
denominations and traditions in the United States. Additional
denominations, representing millions of additional members,
are already in serious conversation about joining.

I believe CCT can slowly help us make progress toward
better understanding, common witness, and—please God—
greater unity. I hope that CCT can become an instrument for
answering our Lord's prayer that the loving unity of his followers would be so strong and visible that the world would

believe: "I in them and you in me. May they be brought to complete unity to let the world know that you sent me" (John 17:23 NIV). We dare not rest content until our life together as Christians represents the fulfillment of our Lord's prayer for his church.

Taking Another Step Together

For much of the last five centuries, evangelical Protestants and Roman Catholics have disagreed, fought, and killed each other. Fortunately, that has begun to change significantly in recent years.

In 2000, InterVarsity Press published *Catholics and Evangelicals: Do They Share a Common Future?* edited by Thomas P. Rausch, which provides an overview of some of the most important recent conversations. From 1977 to 1984, John Stott led an evangelical delegation in dialogue with Catholics appointed by the Vatican in the groundbreaking "Evangelical-Roman Catholic Dialogue on Mission." In 1994, a team led by Chuck Colson and Richard John Neuhaus issued the much discussed "Evangelicals and Catholics Together," which called for cooperation on public policy but focused rather one-sidedly on pro-life and pro-family issues. Three years later, a distinguished circle of evangelical and Catholic theologians signed "The Gift of Salvation," which outlined both wide areas of agreement and points of continuing disagreement. Since 1987, Fuller Seminary and the Catholic Archdiocese of Los Angeles have carried on regular conversations.

In 2000 in Philadelphia, about a hundred evangelicals and Catholic leaders met at Eastern Baptist Theological Seminary to announce another step in this exciting emerging cooperation, issuing a new document and joint effort: "Cooperating for the Common Good."

Since 1997, I have had the privilege of participating in a small group of evangelical Protestant and Catholic leaders, sponsored by the Catholic Archdiocese of Philadelphia and the evangelical Philadelphia Leadership Foundation. We meet regularly to pray, worship, and explore what God might want us to do together. I also had the joy—well, mostly joy!—of writing the numerous drafts of our joint document.

"Cooperating for the Common Good" calls on all who affirm historic Christianity as confessed in the Apostles' and Nicene Creeds to cooperate in turning our society away from the relativism, individualism, and abandonment of transcendent moral truth that is destroying individuals, families, and public life. We also acknowledged that evangelicals and Catholics have often misunderstood, misrepresented, and sinned against each other. And we still disagree on some things—but we've discovered, as the document says, that "the wall of our separation does not reach to heaven."

The joint document celebrates what we hold in common: a belief in the one Triune God—Father, Son, and Holy Spirit—who is the source of all truth and justice, and in Jesus the Messiah, true God and true man; a belief that all human beings enjoy inestimable dignity; and a belief that God has uniquely and authoritatively revealed his will in the Bible. That's a lot of common ground! These and other commonly held beliefs, we declared, offer a unique foundation for shaping society in a way that best promotes wholeness for all.

The core of the concrete agenda announced in "Cooperating for the Common Good" is the balanced program that the late Cardinal Bernadin called "The Seamless Garment" and Evangelicals for Social Action has called being "completely pro-life." Together we embrace a policy agenda that cuts across stereotypes and traditional party lines. Moral truth, we believe, compels us both to affirm the sanctity of human life and to empower the poor; both to seek racial justice and to rebuild the family.

As we work for dignity, respect and equal opportunity for women and men, we will insist upon the legal definition of marriage embraced by virtually all civilizations over millennia of human history. Because we treasure the creation given by the Creator, we will care for the environment and all living species without forgetting that persons alone are created in God's image.

Will anything come of this? Just think of the impact possible if large numbers of evangelicals and Catholics begin insisting that their political representatives reflect that full agenda. Half of all American voters are evangelicals and Catholics. If we learn how to work together in a sustained way over the next couple of decades, we could very well reshape American politics and culture.

Part 6

WEALTH, POVERTY, MATERIALISM, AND SABBATH

They're Still Hungry; We're Still Rich

During 1967, I served as part-time pastor for a little Baptist church in Connecticut. My duties included a weekly sermon. Somehow, one weekend, I decided to focus on the poor. I placed a brief picture of global poverty alongside the biblical teaching about the poor. Since I never like to end sermons or speeches without some concrete application, I needed a call to commitment. (Maybe I have experienced too many altar calls.) The idea of a "graduated tithe" took shape as I finished the sermon that Saturday evening. In the pulpit the next morning, I suggested to a handful of puzzled folk that they should consider giving an increasingly larger percent of their income to charity as their income increased.

I doubt anybody in the service that morning ever tried the idea. But Arbutus and I did. We decided to give 10 percent of a modest base income to kingdom work and then increase the percentage as our income grew. It was easy at first—especially as a graduate student. Even the expenses of two new sons and a modest apartment at Messiah College's inner-city campus, where I started to teach in 1968, fit comfortably within our scheme of the graduated tithe.

In the early seventies, I expanded the old sermon into an article called "The Graduated Tithe" for *His* magazine. That led to a contract with InterVarsity Press for a little book of the same title. During the writing, however, the manuscript grew and the book appeared in 1977 under the title *Rich Christians in an Age of Hunger*.

153

The result astonished me as much as anyone. InterVarsity Press thought the book might sell ten or fifteen thousand copies. That sounded great to me—especially compared with the few hundred copies of my doctoral dissertation that the publisher had managed to sell. Nobody dreamed that thirty years later more than four hundred thousand copies would be in print in nine different languages.

My public identity has been intertwined with the book ever since. In our personal life, too, Arbutus and I have struggled to live in accord with the ideas in the book, including the graduated tithe. And struggle it sometimes is.

From the beginning, Arbutus and I determined to be tougher on ourselves than on the children. So when they came home from school (in about seventh grade) and told us how embarrassing it was to be the only kids without name-brand running shoes, we bought them the shoes (fortunately, we found a wonderful, messy, discount sneaker shop). When Michael came home embarrassed by the patches on his pants, we rushed off to buy him new clothes—at a store called the House of Bargains!

Living in an interracial, lower-income section of Philadelphia also helped. Not only were housing costs much lower, our children's peers also had fewer, less expensive clothes and toys than did suburban kids. So our kids lived reasonably satisfied with our lifestyle.

We were not poor. In fact, we have always enjoyed a standard of living shared by few of our global neighbors. Holding together a delight in the good earth's bounty and a sharing lifestyle has been a perpetual challenge with no easy answers. Distinguishing necessities and luxuries is crucial, but no simple calculation identifies the dividing line. We have never wallowed in guilt. Money and time for tennis, fishing, and long family trips have enriched our lives.

I have learned a lot since I wrote the first edition of *Rich*

Christians. Critics were probably right that I needed to learn more about economics. In the twentieth-anniversary edition I reflected on how my thinking has changed. Yet I still think that God and God's faithful people have a powerful concern for the poor. I also think private property is so good that everybody ought to have some.

After thirty years of living with the varied consequences of being the author of *Rich Christians*, my overriding feeling is astonished gratitude. I am a farm boy whom God surprised with a good education and wide-open doors that I never dreamed of back in my unheated farmhouse bedroom. Sometimes the criticism has been unfair. Occasionally, the life-style choices have seemed constricting. Far more dominant, however, has been the confirmation that Jesus' way is the path to abiding joy and lasting self-fulfillment. I am grateful for the privilege of having my life intertwined with *Rich Christians*. My prayer is that God will give me the grace to live faithfully to whatever in the book is biblical and true.

Christians and Materialism: Is It 'Godly'?

I want the readers of this book to delight in a luxurious Christmas dinner every year. I intend to enjoy big helpings of turkey, mashed potatoes and gravy, and assorted other goodies.

Why do I say that? Because some people seem to feel guilty at Thanksgiving or Christmas celebrations. Some even suppose the author of *Rich Christians in an Age of Hunger* thinks they *ought* to feel guilty. I have actually sat down as a guest at a lovely meal only to hear the host pray something like, "Dear Lord, forgive us for enjoying this good meal while others are hungry."

That makes me want to shout, "No! God loves feasts!" God created a gorgeous world full of splendor and beauty and wants us to enjoy it. Of course we should not overeat every day. And we must share sacrificially with the poor. But celebrations from time to time are *pleasing* to the Creator.

We should celebrate at Christmas because biblical faith is profoundly incarnational. Unlike some Eastern religions, Christianity says the material world is very good. So good the Creator of the galaxies became flesh. So good the Incarnate One loved banquets and feasts and marriage celebrations. So good the Crucified One rose bodily from the dead. So good that when he returns, he promises a feast—the marriage supper of the Lamb.

Please, have a feast at Christmas!

But what about the poor? Am I endorsing the tragic consumerism of so many Christians? Not at all. The Bible calls affluent Christians to share in *costly* ways. We need the proper balance between the biblical invitation to revel in the splendors of the material world and the biblical command to give sacrificially.

Sadly, I fear this balance is lacking in John R. Schneider's 1994 book *Godly Materialism: Rethinking Money & Possessions*. Much in the book is true and helpful. The Bible does promote a godly love for the material world. We must avoid legalism and asceticism.

But Schneider says he wrote largely for wealthy Christian professionals who are "financially secure, if not extremely rich, and most adopt a lifestyle that is more or less commensurate with that of the middle or upper classes" (p. 14). Central to Schneider's agenda is his concern to assure these folk that they need not feel guilty about their affluent lifestyles.

Is that really, I wonder, where Amos and Jesus would have placed the emphasis?

Schneider attacks what he calls my "utilitarian reasoning": "The view that enjoyment of superfluous wealth is morally wrong in a context where others have unsatisfied basic needs" (p. 17). Yeah, I guess I plead guilty to thinking that enjoying superfluous wealth while others are starving is wrong.

But that does not mean that our sharing with the poor means that we too must live in poverty. Nor does it mean that we should agonize over every daily expenditure. And, yes, we will have to wrestle with the word *superfluous*.

Unlike Schneider, I think the general distinction between necessities and luxuries is helpful and important. Granted, the distinction is not easy to make. I understand necessities to include what we need to participate in our society in a joyful, dignified way, including times of "luxurious" celebration. But if we are not living significantly differently—and sharing more generously—than the rest of our affluent neighbors, I wonder if we have really listened either to Jesus or to the poor.

When we get serious about living more simply in order to share generously for evangelism and justice, a difficult problem emerges. How much should I spend on myself? There is no neat formula, no legalistic calculus. What I suggest is a *process*: read all the Bible says, study the needs of the poor and the unevangelized, discuss your family budget with a few trusted friends, and pray—hard—asking the Spirit to show you what to share. Then make a plan, live that way for a year or two, and evaluate. Meanwhile, give generously, revel in the material world, and don't feel guilty when you celebrate at Christmas.

Admittedly, ambiguity remains. I continue to puzzle (and often struggle) over whether this fishing equipment or that vacation is justified. But if Schneider thinks he has escaped that dilemma, then either he is kidding himself or he really *does* mean that we should enjoy whatever luxuries we can afford no matter how many people are starving.

In my 1994 book *Cup of Water, Bread of Life: Inspiring Stories About Overcoming Lopsided Christianity*, I tell the story of Vinay and Colleen Samuel—a middle-class family who chose to live in a poor section of Bangalore. They retained many middle-class privileges, but they also shared in costly ways. One Christmas, each family member decided to share a major part of their Christmas money with a very poor neighbor. They also gave money to a nearby poor family so that the family could throw a Christmas party for *their* friends. The Samuels had enough left to have a good Christmas celebration themselves. Vinay calls this a "sharing lifestyle."

Enjoy the feasting and worship God at Christmas. But don't forget to share so others can join the banquet.

Consumers, Advertisers, Workaholics, and the Sabbath

Workaholism and our preoccupation with making and owning more gadgets and toys undermine our marriages, weaken our parenting, and create a growing stream of pollution that harms the environment.

How did we get into this mess? And what can be done? The Enlightenment is part of the problem. In the eighteenth century most intellectuals became philosophical naturalists, telling us that nature is all that exists and the scientific method is the only way to truth. Because love and justice are abstract concepts but production and income can be measured, our society concentrated more and more on producing and consuming material things. Material possessions and the money that buys them became our overriding concern.

American historian William Leach's 1993 book *Land of Desire: Merchants, Power, and the Rise of a New American Culture*, suggests this explanation for our creeping materialism. The Puritans and other Christian traditions had shaped early nineteenth-century American culture to value thrift, frugality, and modest lifestyles. Fine enough, except that booming industrial America demanded growth, and modesty simply didn't sell enough products. So businesses developed advertising techniques to persuade us that joy and happiness come through fashion, timesaving machines, and gadgets. Diabolically clever ads exploited our weaknesses, seduced us with self-indulgence and instant gratification, and mocked frugality and simplicity.

We even invented patriotic and religious justifications for our preoccupation with growth, so that eventually we all believed that, as John Maynard Keynes put it, "consumption is the sole end and object of all economic activity."

Commercial television now exists as the main voice of this ideology. The average adult watches five hours a day—twenty-one thousand commercials a year. It is hardly surprising that the largest one hundred U.S. corporations pay for about 75 percent of commercial television.

Meanwhile, the market economy spreads around the world. Multinationals own the media, programs and advertising create the lust to consume, and markets and profits expand. Even the poorest kid in India knows that Coca-Cola refreshes. Avon persuades desperately poor Brazilian women to buy Renew skin cream (at thirty dollars a bottle) to help them "rejuvenate" their aging skin—by burning off its top layer. Over and over we hear that happiness and self-fulfillment come through more gadgets.

Christians, theoretically, do not believe this idolatrous nonsense. But we easily fall into the same workaholic trap. We measure our value by how hard and long we work to evangelize, empower the poor, or save the environment. Engrossed in our struggle to "produce," we sometimes destroy our marriages and neglect our children just as workaholic materialists do.

How can we break this demonic cycle?

For starters, *we must redefine the good life.*

It is idolatrous to suggest that human fulfillment comes from accumulating more stuff. Lasting joy comes only from a right relationship with God, neighbor, and the earth. Yes, we *do* need significant material resources, but looking for happiness in our possessions will destroy both our planet and our souls.

We must develop a theology of enough. We must model

simple lifestyles; champion policies that permit people to choose parenting, leisure, and community service over the maximizing of income and profits; and develop an economy that discourages overconsumption. Unlimited growth is an economic Tower of Babel.

Some of the things we need to do involve complex structural change. Others are simple—at least in the sense that you and I could start doing them tomorrow.

We need a break. Both materialistic consumers and workaholic social activists need a celebration of the Sabbath. One day out of seven, we should stop. Stop the feverish production of gadgets. Stop our programs of passionate pursuit of justice. Stop, pray, and enjoy.

I am increasingly coming to see that God's provision of the Sabbath is a divine reminder of human limitations. We have lost the sense of our finitude. Sabbath, when truly observed, puts a halt to our frantic striving to produce and possess—or even to work to change the world for the sake of the oppressed.

Make no mistake. The material world is good—as is our work creating wealth or fostering justice. But God never intended us to forget our dependence on the Creator in our concern for shaping culture and doing mission. The Sabbath reminds us at once of our finitude and our dependence on God. Setting aside an entire day to *not* produce good things or even do good kingdom work but to rest and worship is a statement of faith. It is *God* who provides.

In recovering the Sabbath, we begin to turn away from the mad consumerism that destroys our souls and the environment. Sabbath gives us time to rest our tired psyches, enjoy our families and neighbors, and take delight in the presence of our God—in short, helping us treasure the truly spiritual and become a people who treasure holy leisure over the opportunity to accomplish *one more* important task or build another balcony in our Tower of Babel.

I must confess that this is more vision than reality in my life. I still find it hard not to use Sunday to catch up on some important (kingdom) project. But God would rather have me stop and delight in his presence, listen to his birds sing, and have a quiet walk with my wife. And I know that if millions of us did the same, we would offer a defiant rebuke to our culture's overconsumption and workaholism.

Listen. His word is clear. "Come unto me, all who are weary, and I will give you rest."

A Growing Movement to Overcome Global Poverty

On June 28, 2005, I was in Britain with about forty other American and British church leaders at Lambeth Palace for the London Forum to call on the leaders of the G8 to expand our nations' commitment to overcoming global poverty, especially in Africa. Chaired by Archbishop of Canterbury Rowan Williams, the London Forum called on the G8 leaders meeting in early July in Scotland to increase aid, cancel more debt, and improve the opportunities for fair trade so that the poorest nations can make more rapid progress in overcoming poverty.

Every three seconds, a child in the developing world dies of poverty or diseases we know how to prevent. American, European, and Japanese trade barriers, especially agricultural subsidies to wealthy farmers, lower the global prices of key African products and thus make it difficult for poor African countries to earn their way out of poverty. (European farm subsidies, for example, cause a situation in which every European cow receives a subsidy worth more than the annual income of each African worker.) "This means," we concluded in our Church Leaders' Statement at the London Forum, that "all of us in the prosperous world—governments, churches, the media, and populations—stand under judgment. We believe God judges nations by what they do to the poorest."

Before the meeting at Lambeth Palace, the American delegation met with then-Chancellor Gordon Brown for an hour. Both Brown and then-Prime Minister Tony Blair had been vigorous leaders in urging the rich nations to do more to overcome poverty in Africa. Brown was especially interested in what I and Richard Cizik, the National Association of Evangelicals' public policy person in Washington, said about the expanding commitment of American evangelicals to overcome poverty. He spent a couple of minutes talking to the two of us after the meeting ended. Everyone recognizes that this key component of President Bush's political base could have enormous influence in the task of urging President Bush to do more.

On the day before we traveled to London, the U.S. delegation met in the White House with key policy people preparing for the G8 summit. In that meeting we expressed our appreciation of the fact that President Bush has already done a lot to expand U.S. government foreign economic aid. He has tripled assistance to Africa and doubled overall U.S. foreign humanitarian aid since becoming president. That is more than any president has done in decades. But we urged him to do more so that his record is not just good, but great.

Just before that meeting, I met in the White House with Tim Goeglein, the president's liaison to the religious community, and urged the White House to dialogue more with a wider range of evangelicals, especially centrist and progressive evangelicals, who largely agree with the president on life and family issues but want greater attention and resources focused on overcoming poverty and caring for creation.

At the London Forum, we sensed a *kairos* moment—a special historical time when God moves in unusual ways to move our world toward greater justice. In spite of ongoing theological and other disagreements among Christians, the entire Christian community is uniting in an unprecedented way around overcoming global poverty, especially poverty in

Africa. Evangelicals and Pentecostals around the world are joining with Catholics and mainline Protestants to advocate for debt cancellation, increased aid, and fair trade.

One of the most striking developments is the Micah Challenge. The Micah Challenge is organized by the World Evangelical Alliance (WEA) to support and promote the United Nations' Millennium Development Goals to reduce global poverty by 50 percent by 2015. (The WEA is a network of 123 national evangelical church alliances in 123 countries, representing about three million local churches and 385 million Christians.) More and more national Micah Challenge organizations are springing up around the world to work on this grand project for the next ten years.

We stand at a historic moment of unusual opportunity to dramatically reduce global poverty. Evangelicals are strategically placed to play an especially crucial role. As I look back on the thirty years since I wrote *Rich Christians in an Age of Hunger*, I am amazed at what God has already done—and very excited about what God wants to do through us in the next decade. Let's seize this opportunity!

Part 7

PEACE AND
NONVIOLENCE

.

What Exists Is Possible

Some people are so violent that nothing works with them but sheer brute force. Right?

The Pashtuns—the majority tribal group of southern Afghanistan and neighboring parts of Pakistan who provided the core of Taliban support—are among the most frequently nominated candidates for this category of irredeemably violent. Occupants for centuries of southern Afghanistan and the famous Khyber Pass, the strategic gateway from India to Russia, these vicious people defeated every invader. The nineteenth-century British considered the Pashtuns the most savage warriors they had ever met. India's first prime minister, Jawaharlal Nehru, observed that the male Pashtun "loved his gun better than his child or brother."

An astonishing, often overlooked episode of Pashtun history, however, hints at less violent possibilities. Inspired by Gandhi's nonviolent campaign for freedom from British colonialism, the Pashtuns created the first highly trained, professional, nonviolent army—eighty thousand nonviolent Pashtun peacemakers who refused to kill, even under extreme provocation.

Badshah Khan, a Pashtun Muslim leader, persuaded tens of thousands of his fellow tribesmen to embrace Gandhi's vision of nonviolent struggle. Khan's nonviolent army, called the Servants of God, marched, drilled, wore a special red uniform, and developed a careful organizational structure complete with officers and a bagpipe corps.

In April 1930, when Gandhi launched a widespread campaign of civil disobedience across India, the British responded brutally. Soldiers beat unarmed protesters with steel-tipped staffs. One hundred thousand Indians landed in jail.

Nowhere was the repression as bad as in Badshah Khan's Pashtun homeland in the strategic northwest frontier. When he called his Pashtun people to nonviolent resistance, Khan was quickly arrested. Nonviolent civil disobedience promptly broke out everywhere among the Pashtuns. Bayonets and bullets were the British response. On one bloody afternoon, they killed more than two hundred unarmed protesters and wounded many more.

British brutality inspired massive support of Khan's nonviolent army, which quickly swelled to eighty thousand volunteers. Fearing this Pashtun nonviolence even more than their former savagery, the British did everything to destroy the "Red Shirts" and provoke them to violence. They ordered them to strip naked in public and beat them into unconsciousness when they refused. After public humiliation, many were thrown into pools of human excrement. Everywhere, the British hunted Badshah Khan's nonviolent army like animals. But the proud Pashtuns remained firmly nonviolent.

For the next decade and a half, Badshah Khan and his nonviolent Red Shirts played a key role in the battle for independence. They worked consistently for peace and reconciliation. In 1946, when thousands died in Hindu-Muslim violence, ten thousand of Khan's Servants of God protected Hindu and Sikh minorities in the northwest frontier and eventually restored order in the large city of Peshawar. Finally, in 1947, Gandhi's campaign of nonviolent intervention wrested Indian independence from the British Empire. Badshah Khan's peaceful army of Pashtun Red Shirts deserve a good deal of the credit. "That such men," Gandhi exclaimed, "who would have killed a human being with no more thought than they would kill a sheep or a hen, should at the bidding of one man have laid down their arms and accepted nonviolence as the superior weapon sounds almost like a fairy tale."

The fact that they did—if only for a couple of decades—should caution us against despairing of the struggle to create nonviolent alternatives even in the toughest circumstances. Just-war theorists argue that war must be a last resort after all practical nonviolent alternatives have been tried. Pacifists claim to have an alternative to war.

Surely an obvious next step is for both to work together to train tens of thousands of nonviolent troops like Khan's Muslim Servants of God and the Mennonite-initiated Christian Peacemaker Teams that today move between warring groups in places as difficult as Hebron, Chiapas, and Colombia.

Perhaps Jesus' summons to love our enemies is not as naïve as many suppose. One need not believe that nonviolence can quickly resolve every violent conflict to accept the fact that stunning examples of nonviolence exist—even among the Afghan Pashtuns. Perhaps one or two billion dollars spent on training thousands (both just-war and pacifist folks) for disciplined peacemaker teams ready to intervene nonviolently in the most intractable conflicts might be a wise investment. What exists is possible.

War and Peace:
It's Time to Live What We Preach

Millions of people now know a little about Christian Peacemaker Teams—due to the kidnapping of four team members in Iraq in late 2005. When one member was killed and three suddenly freed in early 2006, newspapers around the world ran stories about these strange peace activists trying to work nonviolently in Iraq. In fact, many commentators were critical.

But CPT's work in Iraq is not the best illustration of its vision. Far better is its work in Hebron in the West Bank, where about five hundred Jewish settlers live amid 120,000 Sunni Muslim Arabs. CPTers have been a presence there for ten years, seeking nonviolently to befriend both sides, reduce violence, and promote understanding and peace. They accompany children threatened by vigilantes, seek to prevent the illegal demolition of Palestinian houses, and befriend young people and frightened Israeli soldiers. (See Art Gish's *Hebron Journal*, 2001, and Tricia Gates Brown's *Getting in the Way*, 2005, both from Herald Press.)

Many people concerned with war and peace overlook an astonishing fact: the twentieth century, the most violent in human history, also witnessed numerous nonviolent victories over injustice and oppression, including the nonviolent overthrow of many vicious dictators.

Martin Luther King's nonviolent marchers changed American history. Gandhi's nonviolent campaign defeated the British Empire and won India's independence; while the British did kill some nonviolent campaigners, only one in 400,000 Indians died. Contrast that with the Algerians' violent campaign for independence from the French, in which one in ten Algerians died.

One of the most amazing components of Gandhi's campaign was a huge "army" (more than fifty thousand eventually) of Muslim Pashtuns in the Northwest. These are the same people we now know as the Taliban in Afghanistan and Pakistan. Even when the British humiliated them and slaughtered hundreds of them, they remained faithful to Gandhi's nonviolent vision.

In Poland, Solidarity's nonviolent campaign successfully defied and helped defeat the Soviet empire. In the Philippines, a million peaceful demonstrators overthrew the brutal dictatorship of Ferdinand Marcos. The list of stunningly successful twentieth-century nonviolent campaigns for peace and justice goes on and on. And they succeeded with very little preparation. (For more examples, see my little book *Nonviolence: The Invincible Weapon?* 1989, W Publishing.)

One wonders what might happen if the Christian world got serious about exploring the full possibilities of applying nonviolent methods of overcoming injustice and seeking peace in unjust, violent situations around the world. In fact, the theological and ethical teaching of all Christians demands that we do just that. All Christians claim to believe what the Bible says, and this includes Jesus' statement, "Blessed are the peacemakers, for they will be called children of God."

Pacifists have long claimed they have an alternative to war. But that claim remains empty unless they are willing to risk death, as soldiers do, by intervening to stop injustice and bring peace.

Just-war Christians (the vast majority of all Christians since the fourth century) have always claimed that war must be a last resort. Before it is just to go to war, we must have tried all reasonable nonviolent alternatives. But contemporary just-war Christians cannot claim they have tried all reasonable nonviolent alternatives in the face of three hard facts: (1) Even without much preparation, nonviolent approaches have worked again and again in the twentieth century; (2) investing a few tens of millions of dollars in training would enable us to develop thousands of CPT-like teams that could intervene nonviolently and explore the possibilities of nonviolence; (3) the Christian church has never done this.

It is time to do it! Think of what might have happened before Bosnia or Kosovo exploded into carnage if the Archbishop of Canterbury, top Catholic cardinals (or even the pope), and leading Orthodox leaders had invited Muslim leaders to join them in leading a few thousand praying, peaceful Christian and Muslim followers into those dangerous places. The message would have been simple: "We come in the name of the God of peace. Kill us if you like, but we will stand between you and the people you are threatening."

A prominent Palestinian Christian has said there ought to be a thousand CPT teams spread all over the West Bank. Imagine what might happen if Archbishop Desmond Tutu, joined by Catholic cardinals and other key leaders, led a few thousand praying Christians from all around the world into Zimbabwe, calling on the government to end its undemocratic action and violent practices. One can imagine parallel nonviolent campaigns occurring in dozens of dangerous, unjust, violent situations around the world.

Just-war Christians do not have to believe that nonviolence will always prevent war in order to engage in a serious, large-scale test of nonviolence. All they must do is be honest with their own rule that war must be a last resort.

Christian leaders (both just war and pacifist) from all traditions should together issue a call for something that has never happened yet in our history: the training and deployment of ten thousand to twenty-five thousand CPT-type peacemakers who are committed to using the nonviolent teachings of Gandhi and King in unjust violent settings around the world. It would take only a few tens of millions of dollars. (The annual income of Christians is over fifteen trillion dollars, so money is not the problem.)

If top global Christian leaders (hopefully joined by Muslims) led a thousand trained, praying, nonviolent peacemakers into the West Bank, the eyes of the world would be on them. Hundreds of millions of Christians would be praying for peace and justice for both Israelis and Palestinians. Media coverage would be phenomenal. Their very presence throughout the West Bank would discourage violence. Both sides would feel pressure to negotiate. Who knows what the Prince of Peace, who is also King of kings, might do in the hearts of hardened politicians?

If Christians mean what they have been saying for centuries about war and peace, then they have no choice. Without much planning and training, nonviolence has worked. It's time to invest fifty million dollars in serious training and deployment. We cannot know ahead of time what will happen. But we already know that unless we do this, our rhetoric about just wars and pacifism has been hypocritical and dishonest.

It's time to live what we preach.

The Way of the Cross: Nonviolent Resistance

For sixteen centuries, most Christians have stood within the just-war tradition. For the sake of restraining evil, protecting the innocent neighbor, and promoting peace and justice in a vicious world, Christians have, reluctantly and as a last resort, taken up the sword. Both in my head and in my gut, I understand this argument. A part of me would like to embrace this position, but I simply cannot reconcile it with Jesus.

I sense that the vast majority of members of Evangelicals for Social Action and *Prism* readers are in the just-war tradition. But today, as we all ponder how best to deal with terrorists and terrorist states like Iraq, I want to tell you why I am committed to nonviolence.

The bottom line for me is that the carpenter from Nazareth was God-become-flesh, and I believe he clearly taught his followers not to kill. Every statement about killing and war that we have from Christian writers from the first three hundred years asserts that Jesus taught his followers never to kill.

Jesus came as the long-expected Jewish Messiah, announcing that the Messianic kingdom of God was now breaking into history and that the Holy Spirit now empowered kingdom people to live the way the Creator intended, even though unbelievers still lived in sinful rebellion. That is why Jesus reversed Moses' easy divorce law, demanding that his followers return to the Creator's original intention for marriage. And that is why Jesus summoned his followers to love even their enemies.

179

Jesus' commitment to nonviolence becomes clear at many points. Unlike the traditional warrior-Messiah, Jesus made his triumphal entry into Jerusalem on a humble donkey rather than a warhorse (see Luke 19:28-40). At his arrest he rebuked Peter for taking up the sword (see Luke 22:49-51). At his trial he informed Pilate that his kingdom was not of this world in one specific regard—namely, that his followers did not use violence, even to protect their just, peaceful leader (see John 18:36).

The clearest text, of course, is Matthew 5:38-48. Jesus is obviously talking not about personal private life but about the public arena of law courts and Roman occupation. Rejecting "an eye for an eye and a tooth for a tooth"—the central principle of Near Eastern and Old Testament jurisprudence—Jesus said, "But I say to you, Do not resist an evildoer" (verse 39). He also told his followers to respond nonviolently when taken to court or compelled to carry burdens by Roman soldiers (vv. 40-41). Jesus was not advocating passive acceptance but rather nonviolent resistance, using words and actions that were compatible with love for the evildoer.

Nor is Jesus' call to nonviolence intended only for the millennium when Christ will reign in peace on this earth and evildoers are no more. "I say to you, Love your enemies and pray for those who persecute you, so that you may be children of your Father in heaven" (vv. 44-45). No, Jesus was advocating nonviolence for the present time when enemies persecute, maim, and kill. Jesus is my Lord. I cannot conclude, with people like Reinhold Niebuhr, that yes, Jesus taught nonviolence, but since it doesn't work in a fallen world we must reluctantly reject Jesus' position. His followers are called to live his kingdom ethics, by the power of the Holy Spirit, in this present broken world.

Some people think pacifists must abandon politics. I disagree. I can argue for what is just and good and appeal to fellow citizens in my democratic society to vote for better laws and policies. I can point out that very often people in the just-war tradition fail to live up to its strict requirements, including the insistence that war must be a last resort. (Have we really tried all other options in the case of Iraq?)

What would happen if large numbers of Christians rejected violence and war? Broad-based nonviolent movements throughout history have proven highly successful. Gandhi's nonviolence conquered the powerful British Empire, and Martin Luther King's nonviolence changed American history. Within our lifetime, nonviolence has won stunning victories in the Philippines (against the dictator Marcos), in Poland (Solidarity's peaceful resistance to Soviet communism), and elsewhere. Furthermore, the God-Man who called his followers to nonviolence in the first century is now the risen Lord, King of kings, "the ruler of the kings of the earth" (Revelation 1:5). Who knows how he might intervene if large communities of Christians chose to love rather than kill their enemies?

I do not pretend it would be easy. Following Jesus has been and always will be truly costly. Undoubtedly many people would be killed, and our goods would be seized and our rights trampled. Jesus' way—the way of the cross—has always been costly. But we should acknowledge too that so-called "successful, just" modern wars have also seen the deaths of tens of millions of people.

I dare to pray for the courage never to kill any being made in the divine image, because I know from Jesus that death does not have the last word. Even if millions of Christians die because they believe Jesus does not want them to kill others, the final word will be resurrection.

Part 8

THINKING POLITICALLY

Can Our Politics Be Christian?

The centerpiece of Christian political engagement is the lordship of Jesus Christ. All who would follow Christ seek to submit every realm of life unconditionally to Christ the Lord. Christians therefore reject the uncritical embrace of any and every secular ideology—right, left, green, libertarian, communitarian, or any other "arian" or "ism." Our starting point will be Jesus Christ and the Word of God.

Affirming the lordship of Christ and simply quoting specific biblical texts, however, will not instantly provide detailed political guidance on specific policy issues. Every political judgment rests finally on a complex set of normative judgments on the one hand and social analysis on the other.

A biblical framework. For our political activity to be Christian, the guiding norms for our politics must come from the core of our faith. But discovering the relevant biblical norms for specific political issues is not a matter of simple proof texting. The Bible is literally a *library* full of all kinds of literatures and themes—histories, commands, poems, stories, proverbs, simple narratives, apocalyptic images—a massive complex of materials written over many centuries. To develop a biblical perspective on political issues, we need the discipline to develop a comprehensive biblical view of the world and humanity. Only then can we begin to understand the specific issues addressed in the biblical texts, including what it says about the poor, the family, work, justice, the dignity of persons, and so on.

Social analysis. By itself, however, the biblical framework is inadequate. Nothing in the Bible talks about global warming, nuclear reactors, or a constitutional amendment on abortion. We also need careful social analysis. That means extensive, comprehensive socioeconomic-political analysis of history as well as everything relevant to a particular bill, politician, or problem.

A political philosophy. It is simply impossible, every time one wants to make a political decision, to spend days or years reviewing the mountain of relevant information and analysis. We need some kind of framework—a kind of political shorthand. This must emerge from our biblical framework and painstaking, extensive analysis of our specific cultural contexts.

In real life, of course, our limitations often demand that we make political decisions without the complete process just described. But the more carefully we seek to derive our normative framework for politics from the center of our faith and the more carefully we search for the best social analysis, the more helpful (and hopefully faithful!) our political activity will be. Both tasks (biblical and social analyses) are too complex for individuals. They require the work of whole communities, teams of scholars and activists, and networks—in short, a group like Evangelicals for Social Action—working together to develop a common vision and agenda.

For Christian political engagement, then, we need groups of Christians to apply this process to every major issue of contemporary political life. That means working out concrete public policy proposals on everything from welfare reform to family policy to peacemaking.

In a pluralistic society, one additional crucial step is essential. Many citizens are not Christians. Therefore we must develop a common language and develop reasons for our policies that are intelligible and convincing to all people.

It is absolutely crucial, however, that we first be able to develop, articulate, and defend our political agendas and proposals within the Christian community. If we cannot, we will inevitably "baptize" secular norms and values and their corresponding political ideologies.

Too many Christians have uncritically adopted left-wing or right-wing politics. The result has been a sub-Christian Religious Right that correctly championed the family and the sanctity of human life, but neglected economic justice for the poor, uncritically endorsed American nationalism, ignored environmental concern for God's creation, and neglected to struggle against racism. Equally sub-Christian has been a Religious Left that rightly defended justice, peace, and the integrity of creation but largely forgot the importance of the family and sexual integrity, uncritically endorsed liberation theology, the sexual revolution, and gay rights, and failed to defend our most vulnerable—the unborn and the very old.

ESA has tried to develop this methodology. We have dared to offer concrete proposals on specific issues. We know very well that any attempt to spell out a specific political agenda must be done with humility and caution. None of us can be presumptuous enough to suggest we speak for God.

But I do believe that God's will addresses every specific political decision we face. In most situations, our only access to God's will for politics is through the painstaking, imperfect process of carefully examining both the relevant biblical data and relevant social analysis. We can make almost an infinite variety of mistakes in both areas. Therefore we never dare claim to have *the* biblical or *the* Christian position.

At the same time, we dare not abandon the attempt to ground our political decisions in biblical norms. *Some* normative judgments will shape our politics, and if they do not flow from the wisdom of Scripture, they will come from elsewhere. Therefore, aside from forsaking politics altogether, we are compelled to propose concrete political proposals and demonstrate how we have arrived at them. Then we rightly advocate such proposals with humble confidence—even as we invite others to help us see where we have not done adequate thinking.

Welcome to another election year!

If I Had One Political Wish

During chicken dinners in the farm community where I grew up, we children always looked for the wishbone. We didn't really believe it, but folklore claimed that whoever found the wishbone could make a wish.

If I had a wishbone for American public life, I would ask God to help evangelical, Catholic, African-American, and Latino Christians learn how to cooperate around a pro-family, pro-poor, pro-life, and pro-racial justice political agenda.

Our society has lost its moral compass. Most American public debate used to be grounded in transcendent moral truth. Of course, that didn't guarantee goodness—witness slavery, racism, denial of women's suffrage, and the near annihilation of Native Americans. It was possible, nevertheless, even as late as the 1960s, to ground political debate, as Martin Luther King did so well, in universal moral claims.

All that has changed. Ethical relativism has invaded popular life. The autonomous individual focused on personal (instant) gratification has replaced God at the center of reality. Whether in decisions about sex, marriage, business, law, or politics, individualistic relativism reigns.

The Supreme Court stated it most starkly in *Planned Parenthood v. Casey*: "At the heart of liberty is the right to define one's own concept of existence, of meaning, of the universe, and of the mystery of human life." Few deny the freedom of everyone to think whatever they like. But does the

Constitution guarantee liberty to act out any belief—even if that means harming others, like the unborn, for example? If this radical relativism prevails, it will become impossible to mount any legal argument to restrain the autonomous self, whether the issue is defining marriage, outlawing infanticide or child pornography, or regulating polluters.

Families are collapsing. Inner cities despair. Racial relationships disintegrate. The poor get poorer. Respect for the dignity of all persons—whether the poor, the unborn, the disabled, or the dying—falls by the wayside.

Politics alone cannot resolve these crises. Nothing short of sweeping revival and a widespread return to a biblical worldview and ethics can save us. Unless our churches change, even the best politics will fail.

But biblical faith will also engage the political. Politics can do some essential things to rebuild the family, empower the poor, dismantle racism, and respect human life.

Can we hope for that from today's Democrats and Republicans? I doubt it. Both parties seem mired in the endless pursuit of money, pandering to sentiment and opinion polls but rarely showing conviction. Those politicians who do stand on their convictions are often captive to ideological extremes.

No, the real hope lies in the possibility that large numbers of Christians would seek for a biblically balanced political agenda.

What then must we do? Catholic, evangelical, African-American, and Latino believers must cooperate. A majority in all these communities, I believe, want to transcend political agendas of left and right that focus *only* on family and life or *only* on economic and racial justice. A *completely* pro-life agenda could prevail—if Catholic, evangelical, African-American, and Latino Christians learned to work together.

Two things are essential. First, an extensive dialogue must

develop among all Christians who affirm historic Christianity to see if we can hammer out some common political agenda. Tragically, few white Christians—especially politically conservative evangelicals—have any serious, sustained dialogue with the African-American and Latino communities. That must change.

Second, we must be ready to abandon present political allegiances in the search for a new political movement that is pro-life and pro-poor, pro-racial justice and pro-family. I'm a registered Democrat, but I will gladly vote for Republicans committed to this agenda. I hope my Republican brothers and sisters are equally willing to seek out consistent-life Democrats.

Some suggest we need a new party. Perhaps. But certainly Christians involved in both parties must begin to send a clear message that unless they start fielding candidates who champion this balanced vision, we will abandon them in droves.

The realignment I dream about will require long, sustained effort. But the majority must not allow a relatively small elite to marginalize religious belief from public life or redefine our society in destructive ways. The public square must welcome all voices—including Christians. There are signs, in fact, that this new coalition is beginning to emerge.

Christians who believe in historic Christian faith will not usher in the kingdom. But we can help nurture wholesome families and bring new hope and opportunity to the poor. We can dramatically reduce the number of abortions, resist euthanasia, pursue racial justice, and seek reconciliation. Evangelicals and Catholics, blacks, whites, and Latinos—together—can overcome the dangers that threaten us.

Could Churches and Synagogues Help?

I'm an evangelical—but not the Jerry Falwell, Pat Robertson type. I favor a *caring* coalition. I'm the kind of evangelical who joined the civil-rights crusade, opposed the war in Vietnam, is a (biblical) feminist and environmentalist, and thinks government should help empower the poor.

But I'm dismayed that secular liberal prejudice makes it difficult for religion to play the crucial role it could in solving our desperate problems.

Everyone knows we are in a mess. Violence stalks our drug-infested cities. Single parents give birth to one third of all babies—two-thirds in the African-American community. Divorce rates soar. How do we fix things?

For several decades now, we have favored government programs. A few worked reasonably well. On balance, things are vastly worse. And I believe that Stephen Carter, a Yale professor of constitutional law, may be right—we should give religion a little more airtime.

When David Larson started his psychiatric career, most of his colleagues shared the widespread view that religion does more harm than good. During his ten years as a research psychiatrist at the National Institute of Mental Health, however, Larson found just the opposite. In one review of studies where the impact of religious faith was scientifically examined, active religious commitment (prayer, church attendance) had a positive impact in 92 percent of the cases. Another review of numerous studies demonstrated that religious faith decreased the likelihood of divorce. Persons attending church once a month were more than twice as likely to stay married as those who attended less than once a year.

Harvard economist Richard B. Freeman discovered that church attendance is the single most important predictor of which inner-city black males will escape the destructive syndrome of the ghetto. When he controlled for a number of variables, church attendance proved a better predictor of who would escape poverty, drugs, and crime than anything else, including income, sports, and family.

There is growing evidence that faith-based drug and alcohol treatment programs are more successful than secular ones. Public officials are increasingly coming to share the conclusion of Anna Kondratas, formerly an Assistant Secretary for Community Planning and Development at the U.S. Department of Housing and Urban Development: "In my experience, religious social service organizations often seemed to have the highest success rates because they recognized the spiritual dimension to rehabilitation that public programs did not take into account."

People in the Judeo-Christian tradition are not surprised that social programs combining prayer and spiritual renewal with counseling and material assistance work better than secular programs. People are not merely bodily machines. A person is a body-soul unity made for community with God and neighbor. Knowing God contributes to better physical and emotional health, better choices, and improved relationships with neighbors. As said long ago, "The fear of the LORD is the beginning of knowledge" (Proverbs 1:7).

If faith-based programs are often more successful than other programs in correcting social problems, then we need to find ways to increase their number and scope. It is silly for the government to continue to invest large sums of money in secular programs that are less successful or even counterproductive.

Perhaps it is time to think carefully about expanding the use of government vouchers to enable individuals to choose the most effective programs. Federal childcare legislation recently adopted vouchers as a way to allow families to purchase church-based, religiously grounded childcare. The voucher system is also used to support Section 8 housing for low-income families. For years, the government has been giving the equivalent of vouchers to lower-income college students in the form of Pell Grants. Individual students who receive the grants can use them in secular, Christian, Buddhist, or Jewish universities—in any accredited institution they choose.

Might it not work to do what we are doing with Pell Grants and childcare for a whole variety of problems? Could we not also give vouchers to people with a legitimate need for state support in job training and drug rehabilitation? Might vouchers be a way, as Washington columnist William Raspberry has asked, to allow faith-based programs to compete with government bureaucracy in overseeing welfare grants?

I strongly support the First Amendment's separation of church and state. I do not want the government to write checks to churches and synagogues. But issuing checks as vouchers to individuals who then may freely choose either faith-based, private secular, or government programs is very different.

This proposal does not establish or discriminate against any religion—not even secular humanism. Baptists and Buddhists, atheists and theists are all free to offer competing programs. Government funds go only to individuals to meet legitimate government objectives to further the common good.

At the very least, nobody should be afraid to run a few citywide and statewide tests of several new kinds of voucher based experiments. Surely secular elites who "know" that religion is counterproductive should welcome this new opportunity to collect objective evidence for their viewpoint. And if

God does happen to be there, and faith-based programs prove more efficient and successful, then why waste our scarce tax dollars on programs that are not working?

The Congress That Stole Christmas

It's Christmas 1995, and I'm angry about what the Congress is doing to the poor.

My morning newspaper tells me that the budget bills moving through Congress will both slash 380 billion dollars from programs for the poor and grant about 245 billion dollars in tax cuts to the rich and middle class. They plan to cut Head Start, food stamps, Pell Grants, earned income tax credits—and give taxpayers earning more than 100,000 dollars a year tax cuts worth 47.6 billion on reduced capital gains taxes alone.

That makes me angry. And very sad. God judges nations by what they do to the poorest. The Scriptures teach that knowing God is inseparable from seeking justice for the poor (see Jeremiah 22:3-6). And "whoever is kind to the poor lends to the LORD" (Proverbs 19:17). When we care for the least, we minister to Jesus himself (see Matthew 25:40). God pulls down societies that neglect the poor (see Ezekiel 16:49-50); God have mercy on us.

Even now, one-fifth of all children in the United States live in poverty—the worst percentage among industrialized nations. And it is going to get worse.

I'm not arguing that we continue business as usual. I want a radical overhaul of the welfare system. The budget deficit robs from our grandchildren. But must we destroy today's children to save our grandchildren?

Why should the poor bear such a large portion of the cost of deficit reduction? Analyses of the current budget proposals indicate that four of every ten dollars of the proposed budget cuts will come from programs for the poor.

These cuts come on top of the losses of the previous twenty years and the growing gap between rich and poor. From 1973 to 1992, the poorest tenth of American families suffered an 11 percent drop in real income. The richest tenth enjoyed an 18 percent increase. In 1969, the richest fifth of American were 7.5 times as rich as the poorest fifth. In 1992, they were 11 times richer. The poorest are actually poorer in absolute terms.

And now, in the name of deficit reduction, Congress wants to trample harder on the poorest of our people. Why not instead tap the 85 billion dollars in corporate welfare the federal government gives to private corporations every year? (McDonald's receives federal subsidies to help it advertise hamburgers abroad!)

Farm subsidies don't get cut much. House Republicans proposed a higher defense budget than the Pentagon requested. And the corporate welfare kings continue to get their 85 billion. Let the poor pay.

The House proposes to cut 42 billion dollars in the next seven years from the earned income tax credit (EITC) for the working poor. (The EITC provides a tax credit, or a direct grant if no taxes are owed, to people who work but earn a low wage. In 1994, a family with two children earning 11,200 dollars got an extra 2,528 dollars.) This program, started under Republican President Gerald Ford, was called by President Reagan "the best anti-poverty, the best pro-family, the best job creation measure to come out of Congress." Yet the Christian "pro-family" political lobbies are silent as poor, working families are attacked.

As welfare reforms require the poor to work more, job-training programs may be cut by 30 percent. Congress is proposing to cut Pell Grants to college students from poor families. In an information society, knowledge is capital. Pell Grants don't encourage dependency; in fact, they do the opposite, rewarding work and responsibility and empowering people for a lifetime. We ought to be tripling the Pell Grant program so more poor kids can get a quality college education.

The list goes on and on—cuts in Head Start, food stamps, child nutrition programs, assistance for low-income housing, foreign economic aid. . . . That this Congress proposes slashing all these at the same time it seeks tax cuts for the wealthy would make Amos and Isaiah weep.

And rage.

Speaker of the House Newt Gingrich called his tax cut legislation the "crown jewel" of the Contract with America. It gives persons earning 350,000 dollars a year a tax reduction of 13,000 dollars. Families earning 30,000 a year get fifty cents a day.

I have no interest in defending every scheme to "help" the poor that the Democrats tried over the last forty years. Some of them were foolish—and bureaucratic and anti-family to boot. We need to abandon failed programs and to find new solutions. That's why I supported Republican Senator John Ashcroft's proposals that could greatly expand the role of religious nonprofits in delivering social services to the poor.

The poor matter—to God and to everyone who obeys God's word. Where are the Christian voices loudly insisting that God will judge this Congress and this generation of middle-class voters by how they treat the poorest? And why are the loudest Christian political voices not speaking for the weakest?

What Congress is doing to the poor is a blatant, sinful defiance of the God of the Bible. And tragically, it is doing this with the support of pro-family, pro-Christian voices.

Needed: An Evangelical Political Philosophy

Just because you are a Christian does not mean you get your politics right. That's true for all of us, not just George W. Bush and John Kerry.

Republican Senator Jesse Helms, for example, was for many years one of the most prominent pro-life leaders in Washington. But Helms represented North Carolina, the country's number-one tobacco-growing state, and as such he regularly defended tobacco subsidies and the use of tax dollars to ship tobacco to poor nations under our Food for Peace program—not exactly a pro-life position.

Miguel D'Escoto was a Catholic priest who became foreign minister of Nicaragua under the rule of the semi-Marxist Sandinistas in the 1980s. Around 1987, D'Escoto traveled to Moscow to accept the Lenin Peace Prize, where he called the Soviet Union the great hope for the future of humanity—again, hardly perceptive, especially in the late '80s.

Examples of Christian folly in the political realm abound. In the last couple of decades, evangelicals around the world have flooded into politics. There have been evangelical presidents in Africa and Latin America and scores of newly elected evangelical officials the world over. Again and again, like many evangelical political voices here, they have been foolish or corrupt or incompetent.

But how does one think properly about politics? How

does one move from a strong biblical faith to concrete pub-
lic-policy conclusions—or the selection of a president?

I will give you a very short summary of my answer in the
hope that it will help you decide how to vote.

Every political decision requires four different components: a normative vision; a careful socioeconomic, historical
analysis of society; a political philosophy; and then some
more detailed analysis.

Almost every political decision is grounded in some set of
values about the nature of persons, right and wrong, and so
on. If you think persons are just complex material machines
that will rot and disappear at death, you treat them differently
than if you think they are created in the image of God and are
invited to obey and live with the Creator for all eternity.
Legislators who believe law is grounded in a universal moral
order embedded by the Creator will craft legislation differently
than those who believe law is merely a set of arbitrary societal
rules created by self-interested power blocs.

While a normative vision or biblical worldview is the essential starting point, it is not enough. The Bible says nothing about
graduated income tax, global warming, or democratic capital-
ism. We need to engage in a careful, sophisticated study of history to see what works and what does not in real societies.

But a biblical worldview and careful social analysis are still
not enough. You do not have time between now and the next
election to spend months developing a biblical normative vision
and restudying history. You need a road map—a handy guide
that boils down the essence of what flows from integrating a
normative biblical vision with extended, careful social analysis.
That's what one calls a political ideology or philosophy.

My political philosophy (which I will gladly change if you
can show me that it does not flow logically from a biblical
worldview and accurate social/historical analysis) includes
things like the following:

Society is much larger than the state; therefore, a good government does not try to dominate or replace all the other important institutions in society like the family, media, business, churches, and faith-based social agencies.

Since centralized power in a fallen world is always dangerous, we must guard against allowing small groups of people (whether a Communist Party or a small circle of very wealthy business leaders) to gain vast, unchecked power.

Since God has a special concern for the poor and summons rulers to bring justice to the needy, both nongovernmental institutions and the state ought to adopt policies that enable the poor to become self-sufficient and enjoy quality healthcare.

Tax policies ought to promote economic well-being, encourage marriage, and benefit the working poor.

A biblically balanced platform would be pro-life, pro-poor, pro-family, pro-racial justice, pro-peace, and pro-creation care since God cares about all those things.

Last, even after developing a working political philosophy, a specific social analysis is needed. In 2004, both Bush and Kerry said that their political philosophy called for public law that allows only a man and a woman to obtain a marriage license. But was Kerry right to leave that decision to the state legislatures and courts, or was Bush right to call for a constitutional amendment to prevent activist judges from demanding the acceptance of gay marriage? Answering that question requires careful analysis of many things, including recent court decisions and changing public opinion. (My analysis led me to agree with Bush on this one.)

Both Bush and Kerry had a political philosophy that called for some government taxation and spending to help the poor. But Bush favored huge tax cuts for the rich, and Kerry wanted to reduce those tax cuts for the richest in order to have more resources to assist the needy. (My analysis supported Kerry here.)

The choices are not easy. I find that in virtually every presidential election, each candidate is better on some issues and worse on others. But no mathematical calculus exists that allows one to reach an easy, certain conclusion. One must think hard, pray hard, and then vote, knowing one may be wrong. Politics remains a messy, uncertain art—even with a good evangelical political philosophy.

Should We Have Attacked Iraq? What Kind of World Will We Promote?

This generation of Americans must make a choice of awesome proportions about the future of civilization. In 2002, a hot debate raged in Washington government circles over whether to extend the war against terrorism to such countries as Iraq, Somalia, Sudan, the Philippines, and Yemen, using our overwhelming military power to install governments more to our liking.

Make no mistake; we can do this if we choose. The United States is so overwhelmingly superior militarily that we can do pretty much what we please for the short term of the next couple of decades. Of course, limitations to our power do exist: global opinion, Russian and Chinese nuclear weapons, alternative European views, and Arab control of essential oil supplies. There is also the distinct possibility that China and India would eventually force a global arms race if we were to trample on their fundamental interests. For the present, however, this country stands astride the world militarily in a way that has no modern precedent.

Behind the intense debate about whether to invade countries such as Iraq lies a crucial question: What kind of world will America promote?

There are two options. We can use our power in a unilateral way for the short-term economic and political self-interest of America (always, of course, with a veneer of moral appeal to freedom, justice, and democracy for all). Or we can implement the moral principles we claim to embrace, strengthening multinational, global cooperation via improved multinational mechanisms in order to create a better world for all.

The unilateral approach is tempting. If done shrewdly, without blatant overreach and with a heavy dose of moral rhetoric, we could probably pull it off for a decade or three. In fact, by unilaterally abandoning the ABM treaty, which has been at the center of international nuclear agreements for three decades and by defying the near-global consensus of the Kyoto treaty that requires all signatories to reduce the devastating effects of global warming, we are already well advanced on the unilateral path.

In the long term, however, the unilateral way spells disaster for all. Widespread poverty will breed ever-more-desperate terrorists. Proud, ancient civilizations in China, India, and the Muslim world will, over time, build the technical and military power to fight back. A global arms race with the almost unimaginably powerful technologies of the 2020s and 2030s will make the Cold War look like child's play.

Tragically, some version of this first choice is likely. If the great American political ethicist Reinhold Niebuhr has taught us anything, it is that powerful people and nations almost always employ one-sided concentrations of power for selfish purposes—accompanied, of course, by a heavy dose of hypocritical moral rationalization.

Persuading American voters to set aside immediate gratification and short-term self-interest (for example, cheap gasoline prices) will require immense effort. In order to choose the multilateral, cooperative option, we must launch a global Marshall Plan against poverty, strengthen multinational institutions like the United Nations, and cooperate in a global effort to preserve the environment.

British Prime Minister Tony Blair called for a global Marshall Plan. Embracing such a plan is the place to start. In the contemporary world, where we have learned how to create unprecedented wealth, tolerating conditions where half of the earth's population struggles to survive on two dollars a day is not only a moral outrage but also contrary to our long-term self-interest. We can and must offer the poor hope for a better future. Nurturing even a few economically successful Arab countries would demonstrate that Islam is compatible with the modern world of science, technology, and freedom.

Blair suggested that an additional fifty billion dollars a year from wealthy nations spent on education and healthcare for the poorest would produce dramatic improvement. That is only about one-fortieth of the present annual U.S. federal budget! Nobody is asking us to do it alone, but we could—with only very modest, short-term economic sacrifice.

We also must temper our proud American inclination to go it alone. Instead we must cooperate much more with multinational institutions such as the United Nations and the International Court of Justice, respecting their decisions even when they frustrate immediate national advantage, building by persuasion a global community committed to freedom, democracy, and justice. That means refraining from attacking other nations, including Iraq, at least until we can persuade the global community of the necessity to do so.

Finally, we must cooperate with, and indeed lead, global efforts to nurture a decent, sustainable environment for all the world's grandchildren. Why not raise money for a Marshall Plan-kind of effort by imposing a carbon tax on fossil fuels (for example, a two-dollar tax on each gallon of gasoline) so the market will create strong economic incentives for alternative energy sources? It is morally outrageous, and in the long run even contrary to our own self-interest, for our politicians to operate as if American drivers buying ever-larger, gas-guzzling SUVs have the inalienable right to gasoline prices two to three times lower than those in Europe.

Will we choose a short-term, unilateral policy to protect our present advantage and self-interest? If so, we will bequeath to our grandchildren a world in which terrorists constantly devise new ways to penetrate our increasingly cumbersome attempts to protect our affluence and in which a global arms race threatens the very survival of civilization.

Or will we choose a cooperative, multilateral path that in the long run will truly benefit everyone? If we desire a more peaceful, cooperative world, American leaders of moral vision must commit themselves to a long, tough campaign to help the American people understand which path leads to genuine happiness and security. Like Moses of old, we must help voters see that they cannot avoid choosing between life and death, not only for themselves but also for people everywhere. Imitating Moses, we must plead, "Choose life that you and your descendants may live" (Deuteronomy 30:19).

Blinded by Fright

When two of Jerry Falwell's former vice presidents and central players in the Moral Majority write a vigorous critique of conservative Christian political activity, we need to listen carefully. *Blinded by Might: Can the Religious Right Save America?* (Zondervan, 1999), written by Cal Thomas and Ed Dobson, is a devastating rejection of the Religious Right's political approach over the last two decades.

Tragically, and in spite of the fact that they make many valid points—this book is confusing and misleading. As Ed Dobson concedes, the absence of a coherent, developed political philosophy was a major contributor to the failure of the Moral Majority. But the muddled arguments in this book prove that the deficiency did not die with the movement.

It is heartening, of course, to hear former leaders of the Religious Right make the same criticisms that many of us have been making for years. America has no favored-nation status with God. The Religious Right neglected what the Bible teaches about the poor and outcast. They unfairly attacked enemies and used manipulative fundraising techniques. The name "Christian Coalition" wrongly suggests a divine stamp of approval for one particular political view. The book is full of valid, important criticism of this sort.

Unfortunately, the overall impression left by the book, at least to this reader, is that politics is largely a waste of time for Christians, who ought to know better because preaching the gospel is our primary responsibility and the only real way to change the culture. As Thomas says, "We have tried to build a strong case for the church to lay down its important weapons of political activism in exchange for the greatest force we have to change the world: the gospel of Jesus Christ."

Of course, evangelism is exceedingly important and can transform twisted persons in a far deeper way than any law. But it is one-sided and misleading to ignore the fact that laws and institutions also shape persons and therefore changing laws is one way to shape the culture. Both inner spiritual conversion and better social institutions can contribute to a healthier culture.

Broad generalizations like "politics is about power, Christian faith is about truth" or "faith knows no compromise—but compromise is the essence of politics" obscure far more than they clarify. Power is seductive and dangerous, but it is not in itself a "worldly weapon" that real Christians should reject. Power is not innately evil or contrary to Christian faith. Nor is the kind of compromise where politicians agree to half a loaf rather than none. What we need is far more discernment in order to avoid the misuse of both power and compromise, finding instead a way to employ them wisely as righteous means to just ends.

Offering either/ors where they should promote both/ands does not help evangelical Christians grow toward mature citizenship. Surely it is inadequate to argue that "we are not called to change the political beliefs of our opponents, but to announce the good news." There is a time and place for both, although Dobson and Thomas are surely right that if we distort opponents' views and demonize them as enemies, it will be almost impossible to share the gospel effectively with them. On the other hand, vigorous, truthful political debate with the intention of winning over those who disagree with us is in no way incompatible with evangelism.

Blinded by Might is sadly disappointing. As former top leaders of the Religious Right, Thomas and Dobson could have made an enormous contribution by combining their valid, significant criticisms of the Religious Right with a balanced political philosophy that coherently states the value and importance as well as the dangers and limits of political engagement. Instead they have reacted one-sidedly to their valid fears of the mistakes, distortions, and failures of the Religious Right. I fear the result is to encourage many conservative Christians to retreat from politics.

If evangelicals are ever to get beyond lurching between excessively optimistic, thoughtless political action and withdrawal/retreat, we will have to do a lot more homework developing a biblically grounded and carefully articulated political philosophy. Hopefully, the ultimate contribution of *Blinded by Might* will be its demonstration of how desperately urgent such a coherent, sophisticated, evangelical political philosophy really is.

The Author

Ronald J. Sider is Professor of Theology, Holistic Ministry, and Public Policy and Director of the Sider Center on Ministry and Public Policy at Palmer (formerly Eastern Baptist) Theological Seminary in Wynnewood, Pennsylvania. He is President of Evangelicals for Social Action, which he founded in 1973. Among his more than thirty books are:  *Rich Christians in an Age of Hunger*, *The Scandal of the Evangelical Conscience: Why Are Christians Living Just Like the Rest of the World*, and *Cup of Water, Bread of Life: Inspiring Stories About Overcoming Lopsided Christianity*. Sider lives in Philadelphia and is a member of Oxford Circle Mennonite Church.